UNITED NATIONS CONFERENCE ON TRADE AND
DEVELOPMENT

MOST-FAVOURED-NATION TREATMENT

**UNCTAD Series on Issues in International Investment
Agreements II**

UNITED NATIONS
New York and Geneva, 2010

NOTE

As the focal point in the United Nations system for investment and technology, and building on 30 years of experience in these areas, UNCTAD, through the Division on Investment and Enterprise (DIAE), promotes understanding of key issues, particularly matters related to foreign direct investment (FDI). DIAE assists developing countries in attracting and benefiting from FDI by building their productive capacities, enhancing their international competitiveness and raising awareness about the relationship between investment and sustainable development. The emphasis is on an integrated policy approach to investment and enterprise development.

The term "country" as used in this study also refers, as appropriate, to territories or areas. The designations employed and the presentation of the material do not imply the expression of any opinion whatsoever on the part of the Secretariat of the United Nations concerning the legal status of any country, territory, city or area or of its authorities, or concerning the delimitation of its frontiers or boundaries. In addition, the designations of country groups are intended solely for statistical or analytical convenience and do not necessarily express a judgment about the stage of development reached by a particular country or area in the development process.

The following symbols have been used in the tables:

Two dots (..) indicate that data are not available or are not separately reported.

Rows in tables have been omitted in those cases where no data are available for any of the elements in the row.

A dash (-) indicates that the item is equal to zero or its value is negligible.

A blank in a table indicates that the item is not applicable.

A slash (/) between dates representing years, e.g. 1994/1995, indicates a financial year.

Use of a hyphen (-) between dates representing years, e.g. 1994-1995, signifies the full period involved, including the beginning and end years.

Reference to "dollars" ($) means United States dollars, unless otherwise indicated.

Annual rates of growth or change, unless otherwise stated, refer to annual compound rates.

Details and percentages in tables do not necessarily add to totals because of rounding.

The material contained in this study may be freely quoted with appropriate acknowledgement.

UNCTAD/DIAE/IA/2010/1

UNITED NATIONS PUBLICATION

Sales No. 10.II.D.19

ISBN 978-92-1-112814-7

PREFACE

This volume is part of a series of revised editions – *sequels* – to UNCTAD's "Series on Issues in International Investment Agreements". The first generation of this series (also called the "Pink Series") was published between 1999 and 2005 as part of UNCTAD's work programme on international investment agreements (IIAs). It aimed at assisting developing countries to participate as effectively as possible in international investment rulemaking at the bilateral, regional, plurilateral and multilateral levels. The series sought to provide balanced analyses of issues that may arise in discussions about IIAs, and has since then become a standard reference tool for IIA negotiators, policymakers, the private sector, academia and other stakeholders.

Since the publication of the first generation of the Pink Series, the world of IIAs has changed tremendously. In terms of numbers, the IIAs' universe has grown, and continues to do so – albeit to a lesser degree. Also, the impact of IIAs has evolved. Many investor-State dispute settlement (ISDS) cases have brought to light unanticipated – and partially undesired – side effects of IIAs. With its expansive – and sometimes contradictory – interpretations, the arbitral interpretation process has created a new learning environment for countries and, in particular, for IIA negotiators. Issues of transparency, predictability and policy space have come to the forefront of the debate. So has the objective of ensuring coherence between IIAs and other areas of public policy, including policies to address global challenges such as the protection of the environment (climate change) or public health and safety. Finally, the underlying dynamics of IIA rulemaking have changed. A rise in South–South FDI flows and emerging economies' growing role as outward investors – also vis-à-vis the developed world – are beginning to alter the context and background against which IIAs are being negotiated.

It is the purpose of the *sequels* to consider how the issues described in the first-generation Pink Series have evolved, particularly focusing on treaty practice and the process of arbitral interpretation. Each of the *sequels* will have similar key elements, including (a) an introduction explaining the issue in today's broader context; (b) a stocktaking of IIA practice and arbitral awards; and (c) a section on policy options for IIA negotiators, offering language for possible new clauses that better take into account the development needs of host countries and enhance the stability and predictability of the legal system.

The updates are conceptualized as *sequels*, i.e. they aim to complement rather than replace the first-generation Pink Series. Compared to the first generation, the *sequels* will offer a greater level of detail and move beyond a merely informative role. In line with UNCTAD's mandate, they will aim at analysing the development impact and strengthening the development dimension of IIAs. The *sequels* are finalized through a rigorous process of peer reviews, which benefits from collective learning and sharing of experiences. Attention is placed on ensuring involvement of a broad set of stakeholders, aiming to capture ideas and concerns from society at large.

The *sequels* are edited by Anna Joubin-Bret, and produced by a team under the direction of Jörg Weber and the overall guidance of James Zhan. The members of the team include Bekele Amare, Suzanne Garner, Hamed El-Kady, Jan Knörich, Sergey Ripinsky, Diana Rosert, Claudia Salgado, Ileana Tejada, Diana Ruiz Truque and Elisabeth Tuerk.

This paper is based on a study prepared by Alejandro Faya-Rodríguez and Anna Joubin-Bret. The paper was reviewed and benefited from comments made at the Ad hoc Expert Group Meeting on Key Issues in the Evolving System of International Investment Rules, convened by UNCTAD in December 2009, which was attended by numerous experts and practitioners in this field. The paper also benefited from an online debate on UNCTAD's network of IIA experts on the issue of most-favoured nation treatment.

Supachai Panitchpakdi
Secretary-General of UNCTAD

November 2010

CONTENTS

SELECTED UNCTAD PUBLICATIONS ON
TRANSNATIONAL CORPORATIONS AND FOREIGN
DIRECT INVESTMENT 129

QUESTIONNAIRE 139

TABLES

BOXES

ABBREVIATIONS

BIT	bilateral investment treaty
DIAE	Division on Investment and Enterprise (UNCTAD)
DTT	double taxation treaty
EFTA	European Free Trade Association
EPA	economic partnership agreement
FDI	foreign direct investment
FET	fair and equitable treatment
FTA	free trade agreement
FTC	Free Trade Commission
GATT	General Agreement on Tariffs and Trade
GATS	General Agreement on Trade in Services
ICJ	International Court of Justice
ICSID	International Centre for Settlement of Investment Disputes
IIA	international investment agreement
ILC	International Law Commission
ISDS	investor–State dispute settlement
MFN	most-favoured-nation treatment
NT	national treatment
NAFTA	North American Free Trade Agreement
OECD	Organisation for Economic Cooperation and Development
REIO	regional economic integration organization
RTA	regional trade agreement
TNC	transnational corporation
UNCITRAL	United Nations Commission on International Trade Law
WTO	World Trade Organization

EXECUTIVE SUMMARY

The inclusion of most-favoured-nation (MFN) treatment provisions in international investment agreements (IIAs) followed its use in the context of international trade and was meant to address commitments made by States in free trade agreements (FTA) to grant preferential treatment to goods and services regarding market access. However, in the context of international investment that takes place behind borders, MFN clauses work differently. In early BITs, as national treatment (NT) was not granted systematically, the inclusion of MFN treatment clauses was generalized in order to ensure that the host States, while not granting NT, would accord a covered foreign investor a treatment that is no less favourable than that it accords to a third foreign investor and would benefit from NT as soon as the country would grant it. Nowadays the overwhelming majority of IIAs have a MFN provision that goes alongside NT, mostly in a single provision.

The MFN treatment provision has the following main legal features:

- It is a **treaty-based obligation** that must be contained in a specific treaty.

- It requires a comparison between the treatment afforded to two foreign investors in like circumstances. It is therefore, a **relative standard** and must be applied to **similar objective situations.**

- An MFN clause is governed by the *ejusdem generis* **principle**, in that it may only apply to issues belonging to the same subject matter or the same category of subjects to which the clause relates.

- The MFN treatment operates without prejudice to the freedom of contract and thus, States have no obligation under the MFN treatment clause to grant special privileges or incentives granted through a contract to an individual investor to other foreign investors.

- In order to establish a violation of MFN treatment, a **less favourable treatment** must be found, based on or originating from **the nationality** of the foreign investor.

In practice, violation or breaches of the MFN treatment *per se* have not been controversial. However, an unexpected application of MFN treatment in investment treaties gave raise to a debate that has so far not found an end and that has generated different and sometimes inconsistent decisions by arbitral tribunals. The issue at stake is the application of the MFN treatment provision to import investor-State dispute settlement (ISDS) provisions from third treaties considered more favourable to solve issues relating to admissibility and jurisdiction over a claim, such as the elimination of a preliminary requirement to arbitration or the extension of the scope of jurisdiction.

In this context, and in order to provide negotiators and policy makers with informed options, this paper takes stock of the evolution of MFN treatment clauses in IIAs. It also reviews arbitral awards against the background of the cases that have followed the *Maffezini v. Spain* case of 2000 that was the first to apply the MFN treatment provision in this unexpected way.

Section I of the paper contains an explanation of MFN treatment and some of the key issues that arise in its negotiation, particularly the scope and application of MFN treatment to the liberalization and protection of foreign investors in recent treaty practice. MFN treatment provisions are used in different phases or stages of investment and can apply to either pre-and/or post establishment phases of investment, MFN treatment can apply to investors and/or to their investments and treaties usually contain exceptions, either systemic (regional economic integration organization (REIO) or taxation) or country-specific exceptions to pre-establishment commitments.

Subsequently, the paper analyses whether and under what conditions the application of the MFN treatment clauses contained in IIAs can be used by arbitral tribunals to modify the substantive protection and conditions of the rights granted to investors under IIAs to enter and operate in a host State. With some notable exceptions, arbitral tribunals have generally been cautious in importing substantive provisions from other treaties, particularly when absent from the basic treaty or when altering the specifically negotiated scope of application of the treaty.

When it comes to importing procedural provisions, mainly ISDS provisions from other treaties, arbitral tribunals have gone into divergent directions. A series of cases have accepted to follow the argument raised by the claimant that an MFN clause can be used to override a procedural requirement that constitutes a condition to bring a claim to arbitration. On a slightly different issue, namely jurisdictional requirements, a number of cases have however decided that jurisdiction can not be formed simply by incorporating provisions from another treaty by means of an MFN provision.

The paper finally provides policy options as regards the traditional application of MFN treatment to pre and/or post-establishment, to investors and/or investments. It identifies the systemic exceptions relating to REIO and taxation agreements or issues that have been used in IIAs to avoid extending commitments made under other arrangements. In recent treaty practice, States may choose to continue to extend MFN treatment to all phases of an investment or limit its application to post-establishment activities of investors.

The paper also identifies reactions by States to the unexpected broad use of MFN treatment, and provides several drafting options, such as specifying the scope of application of MFN treatment to certain types of activities, clarifying the nature of "treatment" under the IIA, clarifying the comparison that an arbitral tribunal needs to undertake as well as a qualification of the comparison "in like circumstances". Options are also given to States wishing to expressly allow or prohibit the use of MFN treatment to import substantive or procedural provisions from other treaties. The last option is to avoid the granting of MFN treatment given the open ended and uncertain application that can be made in the case of disputes.

While identifying options for a new generation of IIAs, the paper also addresses how to deal with MFN treatment provisions of existing treaties that are based on several different models. Possible options consist of clarifying either bilaterally or even unilaterally through interpretative statements, the scope and application of MFN treatment in IIAs.

INTRODUCTION

In 1999, when the first edition of the UNCTAD Series on issues in international investment agreements (IIAs) paper on most-favoured-nation (MFN) treatment was issued, the vast majority of IIAs concluded by States by that time included a provision whereby the parties to the agreements were granting MFN treatment to the investors (and/or investments) of the other contracting party. However, major developments have taken place since then, both at the level of treaty practice and in the development of arbitral interpretations (UNCTAD 1999a).

Although a common feature of public international law and treaty practice, the inclusion of MFN treatment in international economic law emerged in the context of international trade and was meant to address commitments made by States in free trade agreements (FTA) to grant preferential treatment to goods and services regarding market access. MFN treatment became the central pillar of the international trading system, in order to ensure that member countries would not discriminate between their trading partners. MFN treatment has been defined as the "cornerstone" of the World Trade Organization (WTO)[1] and the "defining principle" of the General Agreement on Tariffs and Trade (GATT) (WTO 2004).

Under IIAs, national treatment (NT) is the essential treatment standard that States grant to ensure equal competitive opportunities behind the border of the host State to foreign investors. MFN treatment is used in IIAs as a secondary treatment standard. It has generally preceded in time the granting of NT by host States and comes as an additional guarantee of equality and non discrimination. Early bilateral investment treaties (BITs) would generally not contain NT commitments and countries would grant MFN treatment to ensure that once NT would be granted under another treaty, it would apply also to the investors covered under earlier treaties.

Classical BITs focus on the protection of investors and their investments made in accordance with the laws and regulations of the host country and grant NT and MFN to investors and investments once established. Certain types of BITs, however, and more generally free trade agreements or economic partnership agreements (EPAs) provide also for the liberalization of investment flows. They do so by granting NT and MFN to foreign investors in the pre-establishment phase, i.e. a right to make an investment in conditions no less favourable than those that apply to nationals of the host country (NT) or nationals of any third country (MFN). Under this approach NT and MFN (although more notably the former) are the treatment standards used in IIAs to make commitments to reduce barriers and remove restrictions to the entry of foreign investments and therefore, their application is essential to fostering liberalization.

When discussing MFN treatment in IIAs, negotiators would focus on economic or policy considerations: for instance, the scope of application (to i.e. investors/investments and to pre/post-establishment) as well as the use of exceptions (generic or country specific), including clauses that would preserve preferential regional deals and avoid "free riders" who could seek to benefit from them. MFN was generally considered non-controversial and negotiators as well as investment officials were more concerned by the potential interpretation and application of other rules and standards.

The application of the MFN treatment to investor-State dispute settlement (ISDS) provisions by arbitral tribunals to solve issues relating to jurisdiction over a claim was not contemplated in the negotiation or implementation of IIAs and particularly BITs that formed the majority of IIAs until a claim was brought by an Argentinean investor against the Kingdom of Spain in 2000 (the *Maffezini v. Spain* case,[2] see Section II.C.2). In 1990, in the first BIT claim, *AAPL v. Sri Lanka*[3] (see Section II.B.), the claimant attempted to borrow a substantive liability standard from a third treaty, but since this attempt failed, the application of MFN did not draw much attention.

The decision on jurisdiction in *Maffezini v. Spain* highlighted a possible application of MFN treatment to ISDS provisions and gave raise to a strong debate that has so far not found a conclusion. The *Maffezini* case was the first of a series of arbitral decisions regarding the application of the MFN treatment clause to import ISDS provisions from third treaties considered more favourable by claimants. Some of these claims have dealt with an expansion of the scope of application of ISDS provisions while others, like *Maffezini v. Spain* itself, focused on the elimination of a preliminary requirement to arbitration. Such awards have further strengthened the debate, particularly given the fact that tribunals have been rather inconsistent in their reasoning and conclusions. Consequently, States began reacting or expressing concern about the growing uncertainty.

Following the *Maffezini v. Spain* case, claimants have also been seeking to use the MFN treatment clause included in the basic treaty (the treaty concluded between their home State and the host State against which they are bringing the arbitration) to claim a more favourable substantive protection. For example, they have sought to import a fair and equitable treatment (FET) provision that would not be available in the same conditions under the basic treaty, or substitute a qualified protection provision of the basic treaty for an unqualified provision of the same sort contained in a third treaty.

The universe of BITs, to date composed of over 2,700 treaties, is atomized and lacks consistency mainly as a result from the negotiation process of treaties.[4] So far, arbitral tribunals have taken different and sometimes inconsistent approaches. Therefore the possibility for one IIA to contain looser or more stringent commitments of protection than others is a concrete reality for many countries that have been signing IIAs with different treaty partners. It is important to have a clear understanding of the way MFN treatment clauses have been applied by arbitral tribunals to import allegedly better treatment and then to assess whether this is a desired outcome of IIAs. It is also important to take stock of the way treaty practice has evolved and to what extent States have reacted to the debate on MFN treatment. This would allow States to:

- Make better-informed decisions for drafting and negotiating purposes (more precise scope, wording, exceptions, etc. in MFN clauses);
- Administer their international commitments (through negotiation, re-negotiation, issuance of joint interpretations or other ways such as unilateral statements); and
- Be aware on the arguments that may fail or succeed in the context of arbitration.

It should be noted at the outset that access by foreign investors to international arbitration as provided by the ISDS clauses of a vast majority of IIAs is a specific feature that has no equivalent in other areas of international economic law. This benefit granted to foreign investors is of extraordinary legal nature insofar as it derogates from customary international law, which requires that any acts or measures taken by the State must be challenged before the national jurisdictions of the State. Only after the investor has exhausted local remedies can the State from which it derives its nationality file an action against the host State, but never the investor himself. Derogating from this basic principle of international law comes with strong implications considering the exposure of States to international responsibility and it is therefore not surprising that broadening the base for international arbitration (formed by explicit consent) by applying MFN treatment clauses has generated debate and concern on the part of the States.

It is also noteworthy here to remind that ISDS provisions in IIAs seek essentially to compensate investors for damages and losses arising from acts or measures taken by the State. In most MFN treatment claims, tribunals have been directly applying the allegedly better treatment as opposed to finding a violation and compensating for the damage created by this violation. It may not be within the role of investment tribunals to enforce commitments or secure their compliance. For instance, they could not force a State to admit an investment in the host State through an MFN treatment clause but only compensate for damages if selective and discriminatory liberalization were established.

In the context of international investment, the current debate is not centered on alleged violation or breaches of the MFN treatment *per se*. Instead it focuses on the possibility for claimants to pick from third treaties allegedly more favourable provisions relating to protection standards or ISDS and thereby derogate from or modify provisions of the basic treaty. Such application of MFN treatment has been designated in certain arbitral awards and by some commentators as "treaty shopping". The term is generally understood in the context of investments being structured or set up in a given country to seek the benefits of double-taxation treaties or BITs (more seldom), when in reality the investors have little or no commercial activities there. In the context of MFN treatment, however, "treaty shopping" has been used to refer to the import practice of provisions from third treaties concluded with the home country of the TNC and does not presuppose in and by itself a negative connotation.[5]

International and national frameworks for investment have generally evolved towards more certainty and predictability in the conditions relating to the entry and operation of foreign investors in host countries. The surge of investor-State disputes since the early

2000 and the interpretation of IIAs by arbitral tribunals (although not a formal source of international law) have shed some light on the actual content and practical application of IIAs. In the case of MFN treatment however, the awards have not provided clear guidance for negotiators or beneficiaries of the treaties, rather they have generated contradictory decisions (not necessarily justified by differences in wordings) and different conceptual understandings on how MFN treatment operates. States negotiating and concluding IIAs, policymakers shaping investment policies and investors investing and operating in foreign countries are seeking predictability with respect to the scope of their commitments and benefits. Negotiators need to know in advance which obligations they are in fact undertaking when including an MFN treatment clause in their IIAs. In the context of arbitration, both States and investors would have reason for concern when seeing that the same argument may succeed one day and fail the next. The current discussion regarding the scope and content of MFN treatment is therefore of particular importance.

In this context, and in order to provide negotiators and policy makers with informed options, this paper seeks to take stock of the evolution of MFN treatment clauses in IIAs. It will also look into arbitral awards against the background of the cases that have followed the *Maffezini v. Spain* case of 2000. Section I contains an explanation of MFN treatment and some of the key issues that arise in its negotiation. It will look into the purpose, as well as their scope and application to the liberalization and protection of foreign investors in recent treaty practice and gives an overview of the legal qualifications of MFN treatment in IIAs.

Specifically, the paper will take stock of recent treaty practice and look into the application of MFN treatment to different phases or stages of investment. It will look into the scope of application of MFN treatment to pre-and/or post establishment phases of investment, the various approaches taken in IIAs as far as the application of MFN treatment to investors and/or to their investments is concerned, and the exceptions used to limit the scope of application of the MFN treatment provision, whether systemic (regional economic integration organization (REIO) or taxation) or country specific exceptions to pre-establishment commitments.

Subsequently, the paper will analyse whether and under what conditions the application of the MFN treatment clauses contained in IIAs can modify the substantive protection and substantive conditions of the rights granted to investors under IIAs to enter and operate in a host State, taking stock of recent arbitral decisions.

The paper will then seek to identify in recent treaty practice reactions by States and the way the application and interpretation of MFN treatment has been dealt with so far in IIAs.

The final section will consider implications of the application of the MFN treatment clause and its possible effects on the design and implementation of development policy of the host country. By looking into the general objectives of MFN treatment in the context of IIAs and the overall effects and value of making MFN commitments relating to liberalization and protection among States concluding IIAs, the study will offer options for negotiators in order to match and implement their policy objectives and priorities. The paper will also offer some options from the perspective of the system of IIAs and the way States may wish to address, clarify, limit or further develop the impact of MFN clauses on the system itself.

Notes

[1]   WTO Report of the Appellate Body, Canada – Autos, 31 May 2000, para. 69; WTO Report of the Appellate Body, EC – Tariff Preferences, 7 April 2004, para. 104; WTO Report of the Appellate Body, United States – Section 211 Appropriations Act, 2 January 2002, para. 297.

[2]   *Emilio Agustín Maffezini v. The Kingdom of Spain*, ICSID Case No. ARB/97/7, Decision of the Tribunal on the Objections of Jurisdiction, 25 January 2000.

[3]   *Asian Agricultural Products Ltd. (AAPL) v. Republic of Sri Lanka*, ICSID Case No. ARB/87/3, Final Award, 27 June 1990.

[4]   For an analysis of the BIT/IIA universe see UNCTAD 2010, pp. 81-90.

[5]   See further Teitelbaum 2005, McLachlan 2007, Muchlinski 2007, Rubins 2008.

I. EXPLANATION OF THE ISSUE

A. Historical context

While MFN treatment clauses can be traced back to the twelfth century, they became common features of many friendship, commerce and navigation treaties during the eighteenth and nineteenth centuries. The early clauses were quite broad, applying to a wide range of issues such as "rights, privileges, immunities and exceptions" with respect to trade, commerce and navigation, or to "duties and prohibitions" with respect to vessels, importation or exportation of goods, as illustrated by the examples in box 1.

Box 1. Examples of early MFN clauses

Treaty of Amity and Commerce between the United States and France (1778)

Art. 3.d

The Subjects of the most Christian King shall pay in the Port Havens, Roads, Countries, Lands, Cities or Towns, of the United States or any of them, no other or greater Duties or Imposts of what Nature soever they may be, or by what Name soever called, than those which the Nations most favoured are or shall be obliged to pay; and they shall enjoy all the Rights, Liberties, Privileges, Immunities and Exemptions in Trade, Navigation and Commerce, whether in passing from one Port in the said States to another, or in going to and from the same, from and to any Part of the World, which the said Nations do or shall enjoy.

Art. 4

"The Subjects, People and Inhabitants of the said United States, and each of them, shall not pay in the Ports, Havens Roads Isles, Cities & Places under the Domination of his most Christian Majesty in Europe, any other or greater Duties or Imposts, of what Nature soever, they may be, or by what Name soever called, that those

/...

Box 1. (concluded)

*which the most favoured Nations are or shall be obliged to pay; &
they shall enjoy all the Rights, Liberties, Privileges, Immunities &
Exemptions, in Trade Navigation and Commerce whether in passing
from one Port in the said Dominions in Europe to another, or in
going to and from the same, from and to any Part of the World,
which the said Nation do or shall enjoy."*

Source: http://avalon.law.yale.edu/18th_century/fr1788-1.asp.

**Amity, Navigation and Commerce Treaty (the Jay's Treaty)
between the United States and Great Britain (1794)**

Article 15
*It is agreed, that no other or higher Duties shall be paid by the
Ships or Merchandize of the one Party in the Ports of the other, than
such as are paid by the like vessels or Merchandize of all other
Nations. Nor shall any other or higher Duty be imposed in one
Country on the importation of any articles, the growth, produce, or
manufacture of the other, than are or shall be payable on the
importation of the like articles being of the growth, produce or
manufacture of any other Foreign Country. Nor shall any
prohibition be imposed, on the exportation or importation of any
articles to or from the Territories of the Two Parties respectively
which shall not equally extend to all other Nations [...].*

Source: http://avalon.law.yale.edu/18th_century/jay.asp.

These early clauses were often conditional, meaning that the
benefits granted by one State were dependant on the granting of the
same concessions by the beneficiary State. The unconditional
approach emerged during the second half of the eighteen century.
The Treaty of Commerce signed in 1869 between Great Britain and
France (the Chevalier-Cobden Treaty) is a prominent example.

This trend was reversed after World War I and during the 1929 economic depression, when protectionist approaches prevailed. Nonetheless, after World War II, prompted by new efforts of multilateralism, the unconditional approach to MFN treatment was revived in the context of the Havana Charter (which was negotiated in 1949, but never came into force). It was reproduced in the GATT of 1947, when unconditional MFN became the pillar of the multilateral trading system (see box 2).

Box 2. MFN in the GATT

Article I
General Most-Favoured-Nation Treatment

1.*With respect to customs duties and charges of any kind imposed on or in connection with importation or exportation or imposed on the international transfer of payments for imports or exports, and with respect to the method of levying such duties and charges, and with respect to all rules and formalities in connection with importation and exportation, and with respect to all matters referred to in paragraphs 2 and 4 of Article III,* any advantage, favour, privilege or immunity granted by any contracting party to any product originating in or destined for any other country shall be accorded **immediately and unconditionally** to the like product originating in or destined for the territories of all other contracting parties.* [emphasis added]

Source: WTO.

Today, MFN treatment in WTO agreements extends beyond its original application to trade in goods also to the areas of trade in services and trade-related aspects of intellectual property rights.[1]

Meanwhile, in the 1970s the International Law Commission (ILC) acknowledged the importance of MFN treatment in international law, by preparing the "Draft Articles on Most-Favoured-Nation" in 1978 (the Draft Articles on MFN). The ILC recommended that the General Assembly of the United Nations adopt a Convention, which was however never done. This instrument attempted to both codify and develop the use of the MFN provisions contained in treaties between States. The draft articles explore, inter alia, matters concerning definitions, scope of application, effects deriving from the conditional or unconditional character of the clause, source of treatment and termination or suspension.[2]

The very first BIT concluded between Germany and Pakistan in 1959 included MFN treatment clauses and it was generalized in the negotiation and conclusion of subsequent BITs. In these early BITs, NT was not granted systematically by the contracting parties, given the protectionist policies being implemented in many countries at that time. MFN treatment was considered less problematic (due to the rare use of selective intervention amongst foreigners "behind the border") and included in treaties in order to guarantee a level playing field amongst foreign investors of different nationalities. The inclusion of MFN treatment clauses in BITs preceded in time the generalized granting of NT in the early 1980s and can be found nowadays in the overwhelming majority of IIAs. A sample of 715 IIAs reviewed by UNCTAD reveals that only 19.6 per cent did not include a reference to MFN. After the Declaration on International Investment and Multinational Enterprises, adopted in 1976 by the Governments of the OECD Member countries, BITs and other FTAs/EPAs concluded by these countries would all include NT and MFN treatment clauses, featuring both under the Treatment provisions of the treaty. Wording and approaches among OECD member countries grew apart significantly however with the proliferation of IIAs.

The network of BITs continues to grow rapidly: the total number rose to 2,750 at the end of 2009. Moreover, in the second half of the 1990's, especially after the entry into force of the North America Free Trade Agreement (NAFTA) (1992), international investment provisions began to appear as part of FTAs or EPAs (as of end 2009, there were 295) (UNCTAD 2010).

B. Definition, purpose and scope of MFN treatment clauses

1. Definition

MFN treatment is defined by the Draft articles on MFN as the:

> "[...] *treatment accorded by the granting State to the beneficiary State, or to persons or things in a determined relationship with that State, not less favourable that treatment extended by the granting State to a third State or to persons or things in the same relationship with that third State.*"[3]

And an MFN clause as:

> "*...a treaty provision whereby a State undertakes an obligation towards another State to accord most-favoured treatment in an agreed sphere of relations.*"[4]

In the context of investment, MFN treatment ensures that a host country extends to the covered foreign investor and its investments, as applicable, treatment that is no less favourable than that which it accords to foreign investors of any third country.

2. Purpose of an MFN clause

In the context of international trade, MFN treatment is essential for ensuring a level playing field between all trading partners and is therefore the central pillar of the international trading system.

Likewise, MFN treatment in IIAs is meant to ensure an equality of competitive conditions between foreign investors of different nationalities seeking to set up an investment or operating that investment in a host country. Foreign investors seek sufficient assurance that there will not be adverse discrimination which puts them at a competitive disadvantage. Such discrimination includes situations in which competitors from other foreign countries receive more favourable treatment. The MFN standard thus helps to establish equality of competitive opportunities between investors from different foreign countries. It prevents competition between investors from being distorted by discrimination based on nationality considerations.

The MFN treatment clause is a treaty tool that follows very closely the objective and purpose of the IIA itself. The MFN treatment clause will play the role of ensuring equality of treatment and conditions between foreign investors, whether the IIA seeks to liberalize conditions to entry and operation of foreign investors and/or offers protection to investors and their investments without any commitment to make these conditions easier, more liberal or less restrictive. In practice, the impact of MFN treatment will be quite different if it is used, in combination with NT, to:

- Ensure the right of entry and establishment for the foreign investors and the conditions that apply to the pre-establishment phase of the investment; or
- Ensure that the treatment will not be different for investors and their investments established and operating in accordance with the host State's laws and regulations.[5]

In the Germany-Egypt BIT (2005), the Parties give a detailed list of treatment that can be deemed less favourable within the meaning of the Treatment of Investments article of the BIT. The Parties list, in particular: unequal treatment in the case of restrictions on the purchase of raw or auxiliary materials, of energy or fuel or of means of production or operation of any kind, unequal treatment in the case of impeding the marketing of products inside or outside the country, as well as any other measures having similar effects.

This list of measures – also called operational measures, performance requirements or trade-related investment measures – in the context of the multilateral trading system illustrates the type of treatment that investors can not be subjected to and where the MFN treatment comes into play. The Egypt-Germany BIT (2005) also mentions *"Measures that have to be taken for reasons of public security and order, public health or morality"* and provides that they *"shall not be deemed 'treatment less favourable' within the meaning of this Article"*.[6] As illustrated by box 3, States can treat foreign investors through different types of acts or measures and the MFN treatment clause targets these acts or measures.

Box 3. What is "treatment"?

The most common vehicle for States for fulfilling their obligations under an IIA is through positive acts of State organs such as the legislative, executive or judiciary, whether taken at the central, regional or subregional level.[a] States interfere or affect investors by means of "measures" or the absence thereof, which include the enactment and implementation of any laws and regulations, practice and any form of regulatory conduct.

Under IIAs, States are bound by two sets of obligations: obligations to provide protection and obligations to provide a certain level of treatment.

- Obligations to grant protection to the foreign investor generally combine an obligation to grant FET (or a minimum standard of treatment) and full protection and security, to guarantee the free transfer of funds relating to the investment, to refrain from expropriating or nationalizing rights or property belonging to the investor except if the measure is taken for public purpose,

/...

Box 3 (continued)

non-discriminatory and against the payment of compensation. These obligations reflect principles of international law and the State's international responsibility may be invoked for a wrongful act when "conduct" consisting of an action or omission is attributable to the State under international law and constitutes a breach of an international obligation.

- A conventional obligation deriving from the treaty itself to ensure a level of treatment to the foreign investor that is no less favourable than that applied to the nationals of the State (NT) or to nationals of any third State (MFN). The treatment refers to all measures applying specifically to foreign investors (investment-specific measures) or to measures of general application that regulate the economic and business activity of the investor and his investment throughout the duration of the investment.

Examples of investment-specific measures include:[b/]

- Limits or conditions to participate in specific economic activities or sector;
- Limits on equity participation in local companies;
- Prior approval requirements for the acquisition of equity or assets;
- Prior approvals for the operation of a business/investment;
- Limits or conditions for the acquisition of land or real estate;
- Performance requirements such as local content, trade-balancing or foreign-exchange controls;
- Specific commitments pertaining to employment, research, transfer of technology or investment amounts;
- Requirements to establish a joint-venture with a local partner or minimum threshold requirements of domestic equity participation;

/...

Box 3 (concluded)

- Disclosure of information for statistical purposes; and
- Regulation on grounds such as national security, public order and culture.

Examples of measures of general application include:

- Starting/closing a business;
- Corporate and commercial regulation;
- Taxation;
- Labour, social security and employing workers;
- Acquisition/registration of property;
- Finance, securities and access to credit;
- Government procurement rules;
- Intellectual property rights;
- Competition;
- Immigration;
- Customs and exporting/importing goods or services;
- Environmental and consumer's protection;
- Enforcement of contracts and obligations through local courts;
- Concessions, licenses and permits; and
- Sectoral regulation such as telecommunications, energy, transport and financial services.

Source: UNCTAD.

[a] See Articles 1, 2 and 4 of the International Law Commission's Draft Articles on Responsibilities of States for International Wrongful Acts.

[b] During the last decade the trend has been to eliminate or reduce measures of this sort, as countries have been seeking to liberalize their investment regimes and make them more conducive to FDI flows.

However, as mentioned earlier, MFN treatment has rarely been invoked to challenge the actual level of material treatment given to foreign investors as regards establishment, access or competitive conditions in host States. Rather, it has been used by investors/claimants seeking to import (allegedly) more favourable ISDS or substantive provisions from a third-party treaty into the basic treaty. Whether such a practice is beneficial to the development of the system of international investment law, part of the normal functioning of MFN treatment or within the original intent of the contracting parties is at the heart of the current debate.

The scope of application of an MFN treatment clause needs to be considered both in its subject-matter coverage and in its substantive coverage. Substantive coverage is generally established by the text itself by defining the covered beneficiaries, the covered phases of investment and any applicable exceptions.

More specifically, the scope of application of the clause will depend on whether MFN treatment covers:

- Investors; or/and
- Their investments.

And whether it covers:

- The post-establishment phase; or
- Both the pre/post-establishment phases.

Moreover, this basic construction may include:

- Generic exceptions; or/and
- Country-specific exceptions.

Furthermore, the MFN treatment clause may include specific qualification or clarification in order to provide certainty and guidance so as to facilitate its interpretation and application as intended by the Contracting Parties.

(i) Subject-matter scope: investors/investments

MFN treatment under IIAs generally extends to investors and their investments. However, the MFN treatment clause may restrict the beneficiaries, for instance, by extending MFN treatment only to investors. The approach taken has important consequences given that investors and investments, although directly interlinked, are formally different subjects and may enjoy different rights under the IIA.

(ii) Substantive scope: pre/post-establishment

Pre-establishment MFN treatment covers the entry conditions of investment, conferring rights to the investor both at the moment the investment is effectively materializing and prior to that point, i.e. while it is still in the making. The host State shall accord the covered foreign investor treatment which is no less favourable than that it accords to any third foreign investor of different nationality as regards any such entry conditions (for instance, access to given sectors of the economy or limits of foreign equity participation in specific activities). The obligation applies across the board, which means that no existing or future measures may discriminate the covered investor *vis-à-vis* another foreigner, unless specific reservations are taken by the Contracting Parties. The conditions applicable to entry and establishment will be defined by the IIA and not be subjected to the domestic framework. From the investor's perspective, the conditions to entry become more transparent and predictable, as the entry regime is regulated by the IIA itself and not subject to changes.[7] MFN treatment in the pre-establishment phase seeks to avoid preferential access or a selective liberalization that would benefit some foreign investors and not others. Excluding some investors from the benefit of MFN treatment, could create unnecessary economic distortions to the host State's economy.

By contrast, post-establishment MFN treatment applies only once the investment is established. Therefore, the protection covers the life-cycle of the investment after entry (which is governed by domestic law, regulations, policies and other domestic measures), from start-up to the liquidation or disposition of investments. MFN treatment hence protects a covered foreign investor that has made an investment in the host State, by not putting it at a competitive disadvantage *vis-à-vis* a foreign investor of a third country, in many occasions a likely competitor, as far as treatment is concerned.

(iii) Exceptions

MFN treatment provisions in IIAs typically come with exceptions, some being systemic exceptions, directly linked with the nature of MFN treatment and some being country-specific, for example sectors of the economy where MFN treatment would not apply or measures non-conforming to the commitment by the State to provide MFN treatment to foreign investors. MFN treatment provisions may give rise to the so-called "free-rider" issue that arises when benefits from customs unions, free trade agreements or economic integration organization agreements are extended to non-members (UNCTAD 2004a).

In order to avoid this result, many IIAs exclude the benefits received by a Contracting State Party to a regional economic integration organization from the scope of MFN treatment obligations through a REIO exception. In the case of taxation issues, exceptions target particular benefits arising from double-taxation treaties (UNCTAD 2000a) or more generally from taxation measures. These are the classical exceptions found in post-establishment IIAs.

In addition to systemic exceptions, such as REIO or taxation exceptions, States granting pre-establishment rights through NT and MFN treatment also negotiate country-specific exceptions, in the form of lists of reserved sectors or measures non-conforming to NT or MFN attached to the treaty. These IIAs may also include MFN-specific exceptions regarding areas such as public procurement and subsidies.

(iv) Qualifications/clarifications

An MFN treatment clause may also include specific qualifications or clarification. However, these are not meant to limit the scope of application *per se* but constitute mere guidance and clarification on how the clause is supposed to be applied. Qualifications of this sort are sometimes part of the MFN treatment clause itself. For instance, recent IIAs are putting emphasis on the conditions of application of the MFN treatment clause, for example by defining the method for comparing the treatment afforded to foreign investors of different nationalities ("like circumstances") or by indicating the specific activities within the covered phase to which the treatment applies (e.g. "operation", "management", "maintenance", etc.). In other occasions the qualification may be placed separately "for greater certainty" purposes. For instance, recent treaties clarify that the MFN treatment does not apply to ISDS provisions. An exceptional case are early United Kingdom treaties that define the articles of the treaty to which MFN treatment specifically applies.

C. Legal nature of an MFN treatment clause

In order to facilitate the stocktaking exercise that follows, to better understand the different exceptions to MFN treatment as they apply as well as the current debate on the scope of application (particularly substantive protection provisions or provisions relating to ISDS contained in third treaties), it is important to briefly review the legal qualifications of MFN treatment (UNCTAD 1999a).

1. It is a treaty-based obligation that must be contained in a specific treaty

The legal basis for an MFN treatment clause is always a specific treaty (the "basic treaty") that contains the MFN treatment clause. The clause may take the form of a specific provision or a combination of various provisions of the treaty. Even though thousands of IIAs currently in force contain an MFN treatment clause, it remains a treaty-based obligation. It is a conventional obligation and not a principle of international law which applies to States as a matter of general legal obligation independent of specific treaty commitments. Even though MFN treatment may be rightly seen as a general and constant treaty practice when it comes to IIAs, it is clear that countries grant this benefit and acquire this obligation in the context of a specific (reciprocal) clause contained in a binding treaty.

As Article 7 of the Draft Articles on MFN establishes:

"Nothing in the present articles shall imply that a State is entitled to be accorded most-favoured-nation treatment by another State otherwise than on the basis of an international obligation undertaken by the latter State."

The commentaries to the MFN Draft Articles[8] in this respect are clear:

"In practice, such an obligation cannot normally be proved otherwise than by means of a most-favoured- nation clause, i.e. a conventional undertaking by the granting State to that effect....

... Although the grant of most-favoured-nation treatment is frequent in commercial treaties, there is no evidence that it has developed into a rule of customary international law. Hence it is widely held that only treaties are the foundation of most-favoured-nation treatment."

A distinction must be made, however, between the non-discriminatory content of MFN treatment and the general requirement of non-discrimination contained in international law. The fact that States have the sovereign right to discriminate and regulate the entry and operation of aliens within their territory does not mean that such discretion is unlimited and not subject to international law. MFN treatment, as explained throughout the paper, requires the host State to accord a covered foreign investor treatment that is no less favourable than that it accords to a third foreign investor. It requires a comparison between two foreign investors in like circumstances, being therefore a comparative test not contingent to any arbitrariness or seriousness threshold. Non-discrimination under international law, by contrast, constitutes an absolute standard (it is due no matter how other investors are treated) and refers to gross misconduct, or arbitrary conduct that impairs the operation of the investment. It may involve, for instance, discrimination based on arbitrariness, sexual or racial prejudice, denial of justice or unlawful expropriation.

2. It is a relative standard

The MFN treatment provision is a relative standard, which means that it implies a comparative test. Conversely, absolute standards require treatment no matter how other investors are treated by the host State.

MFN treatment operates in the same conditions as NT and it requires a comparison as well as the finding of more favourable treatment granted to investors of a given nationality as opposed to the investors covered by the basic treaty. For that reason, the standard lacks a content defined *a priori* and it would not prevent or target arbitrary acts where all foreign investors receive similarly bad treatment (without prejudice that other violations may be found).[9] Any assessment of an alleged breach calls not only for the finding of an objective difference in treatment between two foreign investors, but also for a competitive disadvantage directly stemming from this difference in the treatment. This finding must be assessed through a comparison. Thus a comparison and an objective test of less favourable treatment are required in order to assess the violation of an MFN treatment clause.[10]

3. It is governed by the *Ejusdem Generis* principle

The MFN clause is governed by the *Ejusdem Generis* principle, in that it may only apply to issues belonging to the same subject matter or the same category of subjects to which the clause relates. This principle, consistently affirmed by practice and jurisprudence (domestic and international), was highlighted in the *Ambiatelos*[11] decision and later further explained by the Draft Articles on MFN (see box 4). In the area of investment, the principle has been highlighted by the *Maffezini* decision and not challenged by the many other cases that followed suit.

This principle circumscribes the application of the MFN treatment clause to those subject matters regulated by the basic treaty. For instance, the MFN treatment clause of a commercial treaty between States A and B could not apply to or attract a benefit conferred by State A to State C (for the benefit of State B) related to diplomatic immunity or to aviation or to taxation benefits.

In IIAs, the subject/beneficiary is the investor and the subject matter is investment. Depending on the scope of the treaty, the subject matter can be investment promotion, investment protection, investment liberalization and/or a combination thereof. The MFN

Box 4. The draft articles on MFN and the
***Ejusdem Generis* principle**

Article 9. Scope of rights under a most-favoured-nation clause

1.   Under a most-favoured-nation clause the beneficiary State acquires, for itself or for the benefit of persons or things in a determined relationship with it, only those rights which fall within the limits of the subject-matter of the clause.
2.   The beneficiary State acquires the rights under paragraph 1 only in respect of persons or things which are specified in the clause or implied from its subject-matter.

Article 10. Acquisition of rights under a most-favoured-nation clause

1.   Under a most-favoured-nation clause the beneficiary State acquires the right to most-favoured-nation treatment only if the granting State extends to a third State treatment within the limits of the subject-matter of the clause.
2.   The beneficiary State acquires rights under paragraph 1 in respect of persons or things in a determined relationship with it only if they:
(a) belong to the same category of persons or things as those in a determined relationship with a third State which benefit from the treatment extended to them by the granting State and
(b) have the same relationship with the beneficiary State as the persons and things referred to in subparagraph (a) have with that third State.

Source: ILC (1978).

---

treatment clause will apply to the "investment" and/or the "investor" depending on its substantive scope of application and the specific wording. Thus, the MFN clause may only deal with treatment related to the covered person/beneficiary or the asset enterprise as listed in the investment definition.

4. It requires a legitimate basis of comparison

In order to compare subject matters that are reasonably and objectively comparable, an MFN treatment provision must be applied to similar objective situations. Providing MFN treatment does not require that all foreign investors have to be treated equally irrespective of their concrete business activities or circumstances. Different treatment is justified amongst investors who are not legitimate comparators, e.g. do not operate in the same economic sector or do not have the same corporate structure. The MFN treatment clause requires that the host State does not discriminate – *de jure* or *de facto*[12] – on the basis of nationality. For instance, MFN treatment does not impede host countries from according different treatment to different sectors of the economic activity, or to differentiate between enterprises of different size, or businesses with or without local partners.

During the MAI negotiations[13] some delegations indicated that they understood both MFN treatment and NT to implicitly require a comparative context to be applied. Other delegations considered it necessary to specifically include the formula "in like circumstances". Currently, as we shall see in Section II, some IIAs explicitly include a reference to "like circumstances", "like situations" or similar wordings, while others remain silent. Irrespective of the precise wording, the proper interpretation of a relative standard requires that the treatment afforded by a host State to foreign investors can only be appropriately compared if they are in objectively similar situations. However, it is important to note that by not making a specific reference to "like circumstances" or any other criteria for comparison, the Contracting Parties do not intend to dispense with the comparative context, as it would distort the entire sense and nature of the MFN treatment clause.

There are not many arbitration cases dealing with the actual comparison between the treatment two foreign investors receive from the host State in given circumstances. There is therefore little guidance to be found in arbitral awards on how the comparison should be made. However, assessing a possible violation of MFN treatment may be done by borrowing from findings of violation of NT. Indeed, both treatment provisions share the same comparison requirement (the only difference being that under NT the applicable comparator of the foreign investor/investment is a national investor/investment). In this connection several awards rendered under NAFTA (1992) have consistently established that an assessment of an alleged breach of NT requires an identification of the comparators and a consideration of the treatment each of them receives. Tribunals have used a variety of criteria for comparison depending on the specific facts and the applicable law of each case. They include: same business or economic sector,[14] same economic sector and activity,[15] less like but available comparators[16] and direct competitors.[17] Flexibility has prevailed, with the aim of comparing what is reasonably comparable and considering all the relevant factors.

5. It relates to discrimination on grounds of nationality

Both MFN treatment and NT are designed to prevent discrimination for reasons of or on the grounds of nationality. In order to establish a violation of MFN treatment, the difference in the treatment must be based on or caused by the nationality of the foreign investor. After a reasonable comparison has been made amongst appropriate comparators, there are factors that may justify differential treatment on the part of the State among foreign investors, such as legitimate measures that do not distinguish, (neither *de jure* nor *de facto*) between nationals and foreigners.[18] In *Parkerings v. Lithuania,* the tribunal established that, to constitute a violation of international law, discrimination had to be unreasonable or lacking proportionality, and that an objective reason may justify differentiated treatment in similar cases.

6. It requires a finding of less favourable treatment

With the exception of foreign-investment-specific laws and regulations, the domestic legal framework of the host State applies to all economic actors and operators in the same manner, whether foreign or national. It therefore applies to the investor and its investment, irrespective of his nationality. States do not differentiate treatment granted to foreign investors of different nationalities once established and operating in the host State's economy. However, in the pre-establishment phase, difference in the treatment afforded to investors of different nationalities is likely, depending on the treaty commitments made with the home State of these investors.

Treatment is primarily materialized through "measures", that is, State laws, regulation and conduct. The universe here is vast: basically, all measures that may affect the course of business – e.g. laws and regulations on business law, corporate and other forms for doing business, taxation, labor, environment, bankruptcy, access to financing, financial regulation, land ownership, use or lease, regulatory or other barriers to entry, competition, horizontal and sectoral regulations (see box 3). The foreign investor covered by an MFN treatment clause is entitled to receive any more favourable treatment that a third foreign investor is receiving in any of these areas of the laws and regulations of the host State, whether of general application or foreign-investment-specific.

Arguably, while laws and regulations within the domestic framework are critical for the course of an investment, differences of content amongst the various IIAs do not imply *per se* that one foreign investor is being put at a disadvantageous competitive position *vis-à-vis* a third country foreign investor. For instance, while in principle an investor will prefer to be covered by an IIA that includes a FET provision than by an IIA that does not, the mere absence of such provision does not affect the investor assuming that the host State never breaches the provision. Similarly, even though the investor may prefer to submit a claim to arbitration directly than having to resort to domestic courts as a preliminary step for 6 or 18 months, one cannot presuppose without rigorous analysis that such direct access is more beneficial in and by itself, the amount of compensation the investor would potentially receive being based on the date the damage occurred.

Different treatment does not necessarily mean less favourable treatment, and less favourable treatment rests on objective premises, not on perception.

7. It operates without prejudice to the freedom of contract

As was pointed out in the first edition on MFN (UNCTAD 1999a) if a host country grants special privileges or incentives to an individual investor through a contract, there would be no obligation under the MFN treatment clause to treat other foreign investors equally. The reason is that a host country cannot be obliged to enter into an individual investment contract. In this case, "freedom of contract prevails over the MFN clause" (UNCTAD 1999a). Furthermore, the foreign investor that did not enter into a contract is not in "like circumstances" with the third foreign investor that did conclude the contractual arrangement with the host State.

8. It works differently from the MFN clause in the trade context

As noted above, the MFN treatment emerged and developed in the context of international trade before it was used in investment treaties. However, even though the rationale behind MFN treatment in trade and investment may be similar (ensuring equality amongst the actors concerned) its application is not. While in investment the

NT provision constitutes the provision that has driven both liberalization and protection, in trade MFN is the pillar provision, the cornerstone of the international trading system. While MFN treatment in the trade context is linked to the free circulation of goods and services and their access to markets, MFN treatment in IIAs applies to "investors" and/or their "investments" constituted in accordance with the host State's laws. Regulation of goods and services is more specific, targeted and measurable, while investors and investments are subject to a much greater regulatory universe behind the border. MFN in trade applies to "like products or like services" whereas MFN in investment treaties applies to investors/investments in "like circumstances". MFN in trade was mainly designed to target barriers "at the border" while MFN in most BITs has traditionally applied to measures "behind the border" (given that most BITs take the post-establishment approach). In general, the barriers to entry and after entry of goods and investments tend to be of a different nature.

Indeed, "the scope of operation of the MFN standard is much broader when applied to foreign investment when one considers the regulatory nature of barriers facing foreign investors" (Kurtz 2005). Hence any analogy in the application and the identification of a violation of the commitment must be handled with care. Some tribunals have even rejected the notion. For instance, in *Methanex v. United States*, when assessing the NT claim the tribunal found guidance in the text of the underlying treaty and decided that "trade provisions were not to be transported to investment provisions".[19]

9. It has to be interpreted in the light of general principles of treaty interpretation

Treaty provisions have to be interpreted pursuant to the Vienna Convention on the Law of Treaties (the Vienna Convention), whether required by the instrument itself or by (customary) international law on treaty interpretation. Article 31 of the Vienna Convention (see box 5) contains one general rule of interpretation.

Box 5. Vienna Convention on the Law of Treaties

Article 31
General rule of interpretation

1. *A treaty shall be interpreted in good faith in accordance with the ordinary meaning to be given to the terms of the treaty in their context and in the light of its object and purpose.*
2. *The context for the purpose of the interpretation of a treaty shall comprise, in addition to the text, including its preamble and annexes:*
   (a) any agreement relating to the treaty which was made between all the parties in connection with the conclusion of the treaty;
   (b) any instrument which was made by one or more parties in connection with the conclusion of the treaty and accepted by the other parties as an instrument related to the treaty.

3. *There shall be taken into account, together with the context:*
   (a) any subsequent agreement between the parties regarding the interpretation of the treaty or the application of its provisions;
   (b) any subsequent practice in the application of the treaty which establishes the agreement of the parties regarding its interpretation;
   (c) any relevant rules of international law applicable in the relations between the parties.

4. *A special meaning shall be given to a term if it is established that the parties so intended.*

The rule is to perform one single combined operation. "One must therefore consider each of the three main elements in treaty interpretation – the text, its context and the object and purpose of the treaty" (Aust 2000). Under this rule the "ordinary meaning" is not constructed in a vacuum, rather it has to be seen in the context of the treaty and in light of its object and purpose. Even if the words are clear, if applying them leads to a manifestly unreasonable result, another interpretation must be sought.[20] At the same time, "object and purpose" do not constitute an independent basis for interpretation, but are linked to the text set forth in the treaty. This comprehensive approach is particularly helpful when the text is unclear or admits different interpretations. Given that text, object and purpose are interlinked (Koskenniemi 1989), as the latter rest on subjective premises, recurring to the Contracting Parties' intent constitutes a valid (sometimes necessary) tool, especially when it comes to economic bilateral arrangements and party-driven commitments.[21] However, the exercise should be confined to the premises of the text itself so as to establish but not to create content.

In this context, it is useful to recall that MFN treatment refers to material treatment in the economic sphere and concerns the rules that establish the competitive conditions and opportunities to foreign investors and their investments. By prohibiting differentiated treatment as regards the competitive framework, the MFN treatment clause establishes a level field amongst the relevant players and avoids market distortions, favouring a sound competitive environment, thus contributing to the economic objective of the IIA. MFN treatment means subjecting all foreign investors to the same rules and operational and transactions costs they face in their regular activities, as well as offering them the same market access and operational conditions and opportunities.

Whether the object and purpose of the MFN treatment clause refers to the material treatment given by State measures or acts to foreign investors or extends as well to provisions contained in third investment treaties forms an essential part of the current debate about the scope, application and interpretation of MFN treatment in IIAs.

Notes

[1] See Article 2 of the General Agreement on Trade in Services (GATS) and Article 4 of the Agreement on Trade-Related Aspects of Intellectual Property Rights (TRIPS).

[2] The Draft Articles on MFN constitute useful material for interpretative purposes but have also important limits. A substantial body of treaty practice and cases has emerged after 1978, particularly in the area of International Economic Law. Moreover, the instrument is general in its application and does not specifically address MFN treatment in investment protection and liberalization treaties. The instrument was discussed in the context of the ILC's work on treaty law and sought to explore MFN treatment as a "legal institution" from a broad perspective. It also avoided trying to solve matters of "technical economic nature". See Report of the Commission to the General Assembly on the work of its thirtieth Session" (UN Doc. A/33/10) in *Yearbook of the International Law Commission* 1978 [reference: Paragraph 62]. The Commission has been cognizant of matters relating to the operation of the most-favoured-nation clause in the sphere of international trade, such as the existence of the GATT, the emergence of State-owned enterprises, the application of the clause between countries with different economic systems, the application of the clause vis-à-vis quantitative restrictions and the problem of the so-called "antidumping" and "countervailing" duties. The Commission has attempted to maintain the line it set for itself between law and economics, so as not to try to resolve questions of a technical

economic nature, such as those mentioned above, which pertain to areas specifically assigned to other international organizations.

[3]   See Article 5 of the Draft Articles on MFN.

[4]   See Article 4 of the Draft Articles on MFN.

[5]   See further Brownlie 2003.

[6]   Unless otherwise noted, all instruments and BITs' texts cited in this report may be found in UNCTAD's online collection of BITs and IIAs at www.unctad.org/iia.

[7]   NT and MFN are the key pre-establishment drivers. However, there are other disciplines that may contain pre-establishment conditions, such as Performance Requirements and Senior Management and Board of Directors.

[8]   See ILC 1978.

[9]   "...The grant of most-favoured nation treatment is not necessarily a great advantage to the beneficiary State. It may be no advantage at all if the granting State does not extend any favours to third States in the domain covered by the clause. All that the most-favoured-nation clause promises is that the contracting party concerned will treat the other party as well as it treats any third State—which may be very badly. It has been rightly said in this connection that, in the absence of any undertakings to third States, the clause remains but an empty shell." Ibid., p. 29.

[10] See further Dolzer and Schreuer 2008.

[11] Ambiatelos Claim (Greece v. United Kingdom), 2 March 1956 (1956 International Law Reports 306).

[12] There is discrimination "de jure" when the measure formally targets the covered foreign investor. There is discrimination "de facto", when the measure, while apparently being of general application, only affects the covered foreign investor.

[13] See OECD 1998.

[14] In SD Myers v. Canada the tribunal established that "...article 1102 [National Treatment] invites an examination of whether a non-national investor complaining of less favourable treatment is in the

same business sector or economic sector as the local investor..."
See *S.D. Myers Inc. v. Canada*, UNCITRAL, 2002.

[15]
The *Feldman v. Mexico* tribunal made a distinction between producers and resellers of cigarettes; the *Champion Trading v. Egypt* tribunal made a distinction between cotton companies operating in the free market or in fixed-price governmental programs; the *UPS v. Canada* tribunal made a distinction between postal and courier services; and the *ADF v. United States* tribunal made a distinction between steel producers in general and those who could participate in a highway project. See *Marvin Feldman v. Mexico,* ICSID Case No. ARB(AF)/99/1, Award, 16 December 2002. See *Champion Trading Company Ameritrade International, Inc. v. Republic of Egypt,* ICSID Case No. ARB/02/09, Award, 27 October 2006. See *United Parcel Service of America Inc. v. Government of Canada*, Award on the Merits, 24 May 2007.

[16]
In *Methanex v. United States* the tribunal established that "...it would be as perverse to ignore identical comparators if they were available and use comparators that were less like, as it would be perverse to refuse to find and apply less like comparators when no identical comparators exist". See *Methanex Corporation v. United States of America,* UNCITRAL, Final Award on Jurisdiction and Merits, 3 August 2005.

[17]
In *ADM v. Mexico* the tribunal established that ALMEX and the Mexican sugar industry were in like circumstances. "Both are part of the same sector, competing face to face in supplying sweeteners to the soft drink and processed food markets". See *Archer Daniels Midland Company v. the United Mexican States*, ICSID Case No. ARB(AF)/04/05, Award, 21 November 2007. In *CPI v. Mexico*, the tribunal concluded that "where the products at issue are interchangeable and indistinguishable from the point of view of the end-users, the products, and therefore *the* respective investments,

are in like circumstances. Any other interpretation would negate the effect of the non-discriminatory provisions..." See *Corn Products International Inc. v. the United Mexican States*, ICSID Case No. ARB(AF)/04/01, Decision on Responsibility, 15 January 2008.

[18] The *Pope & Talbot v. Canada* tribunal established that "Differences in treatment will presumptively violate Article 1102(2), unless they have a reasonable nexus to rational government policies that: (i) do not distinguish, on their face or de facto, between foreign-owned and domestic companies..." See *Pope & Talbot Inc. v. Canada*, Award on the Merits of Phase 2, 10 April 2001.

[19] See *Methanex Corporation v. United States of America*, UNCITRAL, Final Award on Jurisdiction and Merits, 3 August 2005, para. 27 Part IV.

[20] Ibid.

[21] "...An approach limited to the intentions of the negotiators of the treaty may be appropriate with a bilateral treaty concerning trade and commerce. However, an objective approach, where current international law concepts are considered, is generally used where multilaterals treaties dealing with human rights or maritime territory are in issue, being areas where international law has developed rapidly..." (Dixon and McCorquodale 2003). It also has been said that the MFN clause "can only operate in regard to the subject-matter which the two States had in mind when they inserted the clause in their treaty" (ILC 1978, op. cit, p. 27).

II. STOCKTAKING AND ANALYSIS

As identified in the introduction, the application and interpretation of MFN treatment clauses raises three key issues:

- The scope of application of the MFN treatment clause, both in its subject matter (investor/investment) and substantive dimension (pre/post establishment, exceptions, qualifications);
- The extent to which an MFN treatment clause can be invoked to import better substantive protection contained in a third treaty; and
- The extent to which an MFN treatment clause can be invoked to import better procedural provisions from a third treaty, and more specifically the limits of consent to ISDS offered under the basic treaty, as compared to that offered under third party treaties.

This section will review and take stock of the way recent IIAs address these three key issues. MFN treatment clauses generally indicate their subject matter and their scope of application. The treaty also specifies whether the treatment afforded to foreign investors and/or their investments is circumscribed to the post-establishment phase or whether it will apply to the pre-establishment phase as well. Some IIAs have additionally included qualifications or clarification as to how such treatment is to be applied. As will be discussed further below, only recently have IIAs begun to address the two other issues, and particularly the possibility to import substantive protection provisions and ISDS provisions from other treaties via the MFN treatment clause.

As most existing IIAs only deal explicitly with the first issue and remain silent as far as the two questions are concerned, arbitral tribunals have faced difficulties when trying to ascertain the proper functioning of MFN treatment. However, recently, IIAs are beginning to address the implications of arbitral developments in this field and are formulating provisions that clarify the extent to which the MFN clause can affect the content of the basic treaty by way of importing from or comparing with third party treaty provisions, both as regards substantive protection standards and ISDS provisions.

A. Scope of application of MFN treatment in IIAs

The scope of application of MFN treatment in IIAs is usually defined in the MFN treatment clause. Illustrative examples of treaties can be found that identify the beneficiaries, covered phases of the investment cycle, conditions, exceptions and qualifications/clarifications. Sometimes, treaties will also contain more specific provisions regarding how MFN treatment is to be assessed.

1. Phases of investment covered

IIAs generally take two approaches regarding the entry of foreign investors in the host country: the post-establishment and the pre/post-establishment models. In classical IIAs, the admission of foreign investors is dealt with by an admission clause which requires that the investment be made in accordance with the laws and regulations of the host country. In pre-establishment model IIAs, the right of establishment is granted through the NT and MFN treatment clauses. The decision to follow one or the other approach constitutes one of the most fundamental decisions for the negotiation of an IIA.

(i) The post-establishment model

To date, most IIAs (in particular BITs) follow this approach, under which the entry of investments is fully governed by the laws and regulations of the host State. This also means that the laws and regulations relating to entry of foreign investment may change over time and that there is no commitment as to a level of liberalization of entry conditions or the removal of any restriction or the elimination of discriminatory legislation affecting the establishment of foreign investment (Joubin-Bret 2008). However, once the investment is made, the MFN treatment is afforded throughout the rest of the life-cycle of the investment, which includes the obligation of not altering the framework under which the investment was made through the issuance of new measures that would discriminate among foreign investors.

The post-establishment model is generally constructed through an "admission clause" in the basic treaty explicitly subjecting the entry of investments to the domestic legal framework. The MFN clause will not refer to any establishment-related activity (e.g. "establishment, acquisition or expansion") (see boxes 6 and 7).

Box 6. Mexico-United Kingdom BIT (2006)

Article 2
Admission of Investments

1. Each Contracting Party shall admit investments in accordance with its laws and regulations.

Article 4
National Treatment and Most-Favoured-Nation Provision

1. Neither Contracting Party shall in its territory subject investments or returns of investors of the other Contracting Party to treatment less favourable than that which it accords, in like circumstances, to investments or returns of its own investors or to investments or returns of investors of any third State

2. Neither Contracting Party shall in its territory subject investors of the other Contracting Party, as regards the management, maintenance, use, enjoyment or disposal of their in-

/...

Box 6 (concluded)

vestments, to treatment less favourable than that which it accords, in like circumstances, to its own investors or to investors of any third State.

Box 7. Germany-Jordan BIT (2007)

Article (2) Promotion and Admission
Each Contracting Party shall in its territory promote, as far as possible the investment by investors of the other Contracting Party and admit such investments in accordance with its legislation. Neither Contracting Party shall in any way impair by arbitrary or discriminatory measures the management, maintenance, use, enjoyment or disposal of investments in its territory of investors of the other Contracting Party.

Article (3) National Treatment and Most-Favoured-Nation Treatment
(1) Neither Contracting Parties shall in its territory subject investments owned or controlled by investors of the other Contracting Party to treatment less favourable than it accords to investments of own investors or to investments of investors of any third State.
(2) Neither of the Contracting parties shall in its territory subject investors of the other Contracting Party as regards their activity in connection with investments, to treatment less favourable than it accords to its own investors or to investors of any third State.
[…]

Another approach is to have a post-entry MFN clause but without a separate admission of investments clause. This is the case with the Energy Charter Treaty of 1996 that provides for post-establishment MFN treatment but which leaves pre-establishment treatment to be determined by a supplementary agreement for subsequent negotiation (see box 8).

Box 8. Energy Charter Treaty (1994)

Article 10
Promotion, Protection and Treatment of Investment

[...]
(2) Each Contracting Party shall endeavour to accord to Investors of other Contracting Parties, as regards the Making of Investments in its Area, the Treatment described in paragraph (3).

(3) For the purposes of this Article, "Treatment" means treatment accorded by a Contracting Party which is no less favourable than that which it accords to its own Investors or to Investors of any other Contracting Party or any third state, whichever is the most favourable.

(4) A supplementary treaty shall, subject to conditions to be laid down therein, oblige each party thereto to accord to Investors of other parties, as regards the Making of Investments in its Area, the Treatment described in paragraph (3). That treaty shall be open for signature by the states and Regional Economic Integration Organizations which have signed or acceded to this Treaty. Negotiations towards the supplementary treaty shall commence not later than 1 January 1995, with a view to concluding it by 1 January 1998.

(5-6)[...]

(7) Each Contracting Party shall accord to Investments in its Area of Investors of other Contracting Parties, and their related activities including management, maintenance, use, enjoyment or disposal, treatment no less favourable than that which it accords to Investments of its own Investors or of the Investors of any other Contracting Party or any third state and their related activities including management, maintenance, use, enjoyment or disposal, whichever is the most favourable.

[...]

(ii) The pre-establishment model

Since the early 1990s, some IIAs have extended their coverage to the pre-establishment phase. This is the case with the BITs of Canada and the United States. Moreover, it is becoming quite common to see pre-establishment provisions as part of FTAs/EPAs. This development can be explained by the fact that these treaties pursue liberalization objectives and see deeper investment commitments as interlinked with trade (particularly trade in services) disciplines.

Pre-establishment covers the entry phase, which means that host States may not apply any discriminatory measure between foreigners as far as the entry conditions of the investor are concerned. This has a major implication: host States are not only prevented from applying any existing measure which is inconsistent with MFN treatment but also from creating a new one. In other words, under this model the host State accepts a certain limit on its sovereignty to regulate foreign investment. Given these far-reaching effects pre-establishment commitments are normally accompanied with specific country exceptions (through a "negative" or "positive" list approach[1]) as opposed to the post-establishment model. Pre-establishment grants rights to pre-investors, i.e. investors who seek to establish an investment or are in the process of making it. It is worth noting that when MFN treatment is granted at the pre-establishment stage, it also applies to the post-establishment phase, this approach in fact covers the whole life cycle of the investment (see box 9).

There are variations as to liberalization commitments, notably when it comes to economic integration arrangements or regional agreements on investment. Under Article 23 of the European Free Trade Association (EFTA), for instance, EFTA members are allowed to set out exceptions to the right of establishment but shall endeavour to gradually remove discriminatory measures. Other treaties such as the one concluded between the EU and Morocco

(2000) simply provide for future liberalization without actually making any commitment at the time of entry into force (see box 10).

Box 9. FTA between Central America, the Dominican Republic and the United States of America (CAFTA) (2004)

Article 10.4: Most-Favored-Nation Treatment

1. Each Party shall accord to investors of another Party treatment no less favorable than that it accords, in like circumstances, to investors of any other Party or of any non-Party with respect to the **establishment, acquisition, expansion, management, conduct, operation, and sale or other disposition of** *investments in its territory.*

2. Each Party shall accord to covered investments treatment no less favorable than that it accords, in like circumstances, to investments in its territory of investors of any other Party or of any non-Party with respect to **the establishment, acquisition, expansion, management, conduct, operation, and sale or other disposition of investments.**[Emphasis added]

---

2. Investments and/or investors

The application of an IIA is delimited by time, geography and subject-matter. The subject-matter application is determined by the terms "investors" and "investments", and the same goes for the MFN treatment clause. In classical BITs "investments" are defined through illustrative asset-based lists that include different forms in which foreign assets may be materialized in the host State, for instance a local company or branch, equity participation, loans, tangible or intangible property, intellectual property rights or economic benefits arising from the commitment of capital. "Investors" are the individuals and legal persons who are nationals of the Contracting Party that is not the host State, owning or controlling the investment. Generally, such legal persons are defined broadly, including not only commercial corporations but also non-profit organizations and contractual arrangements such as trusts and joint ventures. Moreover, the nationality of legal persons tends to be defined under formal criteria, such as the place of constitution and not by the ultimate origin of capital (UNCTAD 1999b and 2004b, UNCTAD forthcoming).

Box 10. Association Agreement between the European Union and Morocco (1996)

Article 31

1. The Parties agree to widen the scope of this Agreement to cover the right of establishment of one Party's firms on the territory of the other and liberalisation of the provision of services by one Party's firms to consumers of services in the other.

2. The Association Council will make recommendations for achieving the objective described in paragraph 1.

In making such recommendations, the Association Council will take account of past experience of implementation of reciprocal most-favoured-nation treatment and of the respective obligations of each Party under the General Agreement on Trade in Services annexed to the Agreement establishing the WTO, hereinafter referred to as the 'GATS', particularly those in Article V of the latter.

3. The Association Council will make a first assessment of the achievement of this objective no later than five years after this Agreement enters into force.

There are important implications of whether MFN treatment covers both investors and investments: State measures may affect one or both categories, individually or jointly. There may be measures affecting the investment but not the investor, affecting the investor but not the investment or affecting both.

Most MFN treatment clauses apply to both investors and investments, because in that way the protection and promotion objectives are truly achieved. However, that is not always the case, as some IIAs cover only investments (see box 11). This would have the consequence of excluding foreign individuals or companies from MFN treatment and limiting it to the locally established juridical person constituted in the host State or assets acquired under the legislation of the host State.

Box 11. Australia-Uruguay BIT (2002)

Article 4
Most-favoured-nation provision

*Each Party shall at all times treat **investments** in its own territory on a basis no less favourable than that accorded to investments of investors of any third country, provided that a Party shall not be obliged to extend to investments any treatment, preference or privilege resulting from:* […]. [Emphasis added]

Another formulation found in IIAs is to subject MFN treatment to the "laws and regulations" of the host State. By doing so the Contracting Parties substantially ease the commitment given that the investment shall be bound not only by the conditions of entry but also by any new measure issued in the form of a law or regulation by the host State (see box 12).

3. Exceptions

An MFN clause in admission-type IIAs comes with few but rather standard exceptions. An MFN clause in a pre-establishment type IIA comes with more exceptions as they include country specific exceptions. In multilateral agreements (such as the GATS), the commitments undertaken by the signatories are not that far-reaching, which is reflected in the greater number of exceptions and general carve-outs.

Box 12. China-Latvia BIT (2006)

Article 3
Treatment of Investment

[…]

2. *Without prejudice to its laws and regulations, each Contracting party shall accord to investments and activities with such investments by the investors of the other Contraction Party treatment not less favorable than that accorded to the investments and associated activities by its own investors.*

3. *Neither Contracting Party shall subject investments and activities associated with such investments by the investors of the other Contracting Party to treatment less favorable than that accorded to the investments and associated activities by the investors of any third State.* […]

MFN treatment clauses may also be subjected to general exceptions, that is, exceptions applicable to the whole IIA. Examples of general exceptions include: public order and morals, national security, and emergency exceptions and the denial of benefits clause. These clauses delimit the scope of the treaty as such. Thus they will not be discussed here. The scope and application of these general exceptions in relation to the MFN treatment is duly explained in the first edition of this paper and the analysis given there can still be referred to (UNCTAD 1999a).

(i) Post-establishment exceptions

Practice continues to be fairly standard when it comes to the post-establishment model. This approach does not include country-specific exceptions (i.e. economic sectors or activities) given that the host State retains control over the entry regime. However, there are two general exceptions that can be found in almost every single IIA of this type, particularly in BITs.

The first refers to the benefits or privileges granted by a State by virtue of free trade agreements, customs unions, labour integration markets or any other sort of regional economic arrangements. This REIO exception is also used in the trade context (see article XXIV of the GATT and Article V of the GATS). Without such exception, the MFN treatment clause would oblige the REIO members to unilaterally grant investors from non-member countries all the privileges deriving from REIO membership (UNCTAD 2004a).

The second exception refers to international agreements that partly or mainly deal with taxation issues. At times, domestic taxation law is also listed as an exception. The reason is that under double-taxation treaties, the contracting parties partly renounce, on a mutual basis, their right to tax investors located in their territories in order to avoid double taxation. Each contracting party therefore waives its taxation rights only if the other contracting party undertakes the same commitment (UNCTAD 2000a). The Czech Republic-Paraguay BIT (2000) and the Egypt-Germany BIT (2005) exemplify the use of both exceptions (see boxes 13 and 14).

Box 13. Czech Republic-Paraguay BIT (2000)

Article 4
National and Most-Favoured-Nation Treatment

[...]

3. The treatment of the most favored nation, shall not be applied to the privileges which one Contracting Party grants to the investor of a third State in pursuance of its participation to a free trade zone, customs union, similar international agreements to such unions or

/...

Box 13 (concluded)

institutions, common market, monetary unions or other forms of regional agreements to which each Contracting Party is a party or may become a party.

4. The treatment granted by this Article does not refer to the advantages that one of the Contracting Parties grants to the investor of a third State as a result of an agreement to avoid the double taxation or other agreements relating to taxation matters.[...]

Box 14. Egypt-Germany BIT (2005)

Article 3(4)
Issues of taxation on income and on capital shall be dealt with in accordance with the relevant agreement for the avoidance of double taxation with respect to taxes on income and capital between the Contracting States. In case there is no such double taxation agreement between the Contracting States, the respective national tax law shall be applicable. The treatment granted under this Article shall also not relate to advantages which either Contracting State accords to investors of third States by virtue of a double taxation agreement or other agreements regarding matters of taxation.

(ii) Pre-establishment exceptions

When pre-establishment rights are granted, IIAs usually contain more exceptions whether generic, classified by topic, or country-specific, classified by activity. The reason is that States may have a number of potentially inconsistent measures as regards entry conditions. Moreover, States may wish to preserve flexibility for future development and regulatory policies (UNCTAD 2000b and 2006) The Canadian approach, which may be found in recent FTAs/EPAs, offers an example. Article 9 of Canada's model BIT

(2004) establishes that the MFN treatment clause (as well as NT, senior management and board of directors and performance requirements): *"shall not apply to (a) any existing non-conforming measure that is maintained by (i) a Party at the national level, as set out in its Schedule to Annex I, or (ii) a sub-national government."* Although most inconsistent measures generally refer to NT, there may be a few that relate to MFN (e.g. sectors regulated under reciprocity considerations). These exceptions must be consistent with the domestic framework and reflect existing non-conforming measures. Moreover, Article 9 establishes that the same provisions shall not apply to any measure with respect to sectors, sub-sectors or activities as set out in Annex II ("Future measures"). Here, the exceptions do not necessarily reflect domestic law but allows some flexibility that the Contracting Parties wishes to retain with respect to said sectors, sub-sectors or activities. These Annexes are both subject to negotiation.

The model BIT establishes exceptions to MFN, NT and senior management and board of directors in connection with the following topics: intellectual property rights, public procurement, subsidies or grants and financial services. Moreover, in the Canadian approach, MFN treatment does not apply to agreements or with respect to sectors set out in its annex III (see boxes 15 and 16).

Box 15. Canada model BIT (2004)

Article 9
Reservations and Exceptions
"1. Articles 3, 4, 6 and 7 shall not apply to:
    (a) any existing non-conforming measure that is maintained by
        (i) a Party at the national level, as set out in its Schedule to Annex I, or

        /...

Box 15 (concluded)

    (ii) a sub-national government;
(b-c) [...]

2. Articles 3, 4, 6 and 7 shall not apply to any measure that a Party adopts or maintains with respect to sectors, subsectors or activities, as set out in its schedule to Annex II.

3. Article 4 shall not apply to treatment accorded by a Party pursuant to agreements, or with respect to sectors, set out in its schedule to Annex III.

4. In respect of intellectual property rights, a Party may derogate from Articles 3 and 4 in a manner that is consistent with the WTO Agreement.

5. The provisions of Articles 3, 4 and 6 of this Agreement shall not apply to:
    (a) procurement by a Party or state enterprise;
    (b) subsidies or grants provided by a Party or a state enterprise, including government-supported loans, guarantees and insurance;

6. [...]

7. The provisions of Article 4 of this Agreement shall not apply to financial services.

There are variations in treaties and in approaches. In some examples, Contracting Parties wish to confirm the application of the MFN treatment clause to existing arrangements (see box 17).

Box 16. Canada-Peru FTA (2008)
(Annex II Schedule of Canada)

Type of reservation: MFN (Article 804)

Canada reserves the right to adopt or maintain any measure that accords differential treatment to countries under any bilateral or multilateral international agreements in force or signed prior to the date of entry into force of this Agreement.

Canada reserves the right to adopt or maintain any measure that accords differential treatment to a country pursuant to any existing or future bilateral or multilateral agreement relating to:

a) aviation;
b) fisheries;
c) maritime matters, including salvage.

Box 17. ASEAN Comprehensive Investment Agreement (2009)

Article 6
Most-Favoured-Nation Treatment (Footnote 4)
Footnote 4:
For greater certainty:

    (a) […]

    (b) in relation to investments falling within the scope of this Agreement, any preferential treatment granted by a Member State to investors of any other Member State or a non- Member State and to their investments, under any existing or future agreements or arrangements to which a Member State is a party shall be extended on a most-favoured-nation basis to all Member States.

Exceptions also play a critical role for liberalization strategies. States may wish to retain control of any liberalization with third treaty partners and not extend it automatically via MFN treatment. For instance, the Japan-Switzerland EPA (2009) establishes that the MFN clause does not apply to third treaties providing for substantial liberalization of investment; in case such liberalization occurs, it would be subject to consultation with a view of incorporating it into the basic treaty (see box 18).

Box 18. Japan-Switzerland EPA (2009)

Article 88 Most-Favoured-Nation Treatment

[...]

3. If a Party accords more favourable treatment to investors of a non-Party and their investments by concluding or amending a free trade agreement, customs union or similar agreement that provides for substantial liberalisation of investment, it shall not be obliged to accord such treatment to investors of the other Party and their investments. Any such treatment accorded by a Party shall be notified to the other Party without delay and the former Party shall endeavour to accord to investors of the latter Party and their investments treatment no less favourable than that accorded under the concluded or amended agreement. The former Party, upon request by the latter Party, shall enter into negotiations with a view to incorporating into this Agreement treatment no less favourable than that accorded under such concluded or amended agreement.

Other IIAs have taken a specific range of exceptions designed to cover special situations found in the Contracting Parties public policies. For instance, the China-Peru FTA (2009) has excepted from the MFN treatment clause socially or economically disadvantaged minorities and ethnic groups, as well as cultural industries related to the production of books, magazines, periodical publications, or printed or electronic newspapers and music scores (see box 19).

Box 19. China-Peru FTA (2009)

Article 131 Most-Favoured-Nation Treatment

1. Each Party shall accord to investors of the other Party treatment no less favourable than that it accords, in like circumstances, to investors of any third State with respect to the establishment, acquisition, expansion, management, conduct, operation, and sale or other disposition of investments in its territory.

[…]

3. Notwithstanding paragraphs 1 and 2, the Parties reserve the right to adopt or maintain any measure that accords differential treatment:

(a) to socially or economically disadvantaged minorities and ethnic groups; or

b) involving cultural industries related to the production of books, magazines, periodical publications, or printed or electronic newspapers and music scores.

---

4. Conditions and qualifications

(i) "Like circumstances" or "like situations"

As outlined above, the MFN treatment obligation does not mean that foreign investors have to be treated equally irrespective of their concrete activity or circumstance. Different treatment is justified if the would-be comparators are in different objective situations. This requires comparing what is reasonably comparable. Some treaties refer to "like circumstances", "like situations" or similar wording. This is the case with the NAFTA (1992), the United States model BIT (2004), the Canadian model BIT (2004), BITs concluded by Mexico and many recent FTAs/EPAs. Many classical BITs do not include any such comparison formula. However, the absence thereof does not mean that the contracting parties to such treaties intended that the standard be applied without a proper comparison. This comparison formula has to be seen as an implicit component of MFN treatment, although for purposes of greater certainty and according to the legal tradition of some countries, it may be preferable to make it explicit.

(ii) Specific investment related activities covered by the MFN treatment clause

MFN treatment applies to the treatment afforded by the host State, as applicable, to investors and/or their investment, during the post-establishment or pre/post-establishment phases. As mentioned above, this treatment covers the life-cycle of the investment as regulated by the host State's laws and regulations. However, some MFN clauses are more precise than others.

Some MFN clauses, specifically those applying to pre-establishment, link the treatment to a closed set of activities (sometimes for both investors/investments or only for investments) (see box 20).

This list of investment activities includes pre- or post-establishment activities. Hence, special attention must be paid in order to reach the intended effect. Pre-establishment activities typically include the "establishment, acquisition and expansion" of investments, whereas post-establishment activities include the "management, maintenance, conduct, operation, use, enjoyment, sell, disposal or disposition" of investments. Expansion of investment that is subject to prior approval or other authorization may be considered part of the post-establishment activities by some countries.

Box 20. Japan-Malaysia EPA (2006)
Article 76   **Most-Favoured-Nation Treatment**   *Each Country shall accord to investors of the other Country and to their investments treatment no less favourable than that it accords in like circumstances to investors of a third State and to their investments, with respect to investment activities.*   *'Investment activities' being defined in Article 75 as "establishment, acquisition, expansion, management, operation, maintenance, use, possession, liquidation, sale, or other disposition of investments".*

Other MFN treatment clauses do not refer to any specific activity, but to the "treatment" in general owed to investors and/or their investments (box 21). However, this wording does not necessarily mean that the MFN treatment should be applied broadly as compared to the first approach. Out of the explicit indication of the IIA's entry model approach, the inclusion of investment-related activities may reflect both intent of the Contracting Parties to restrict MFN treatment or merely an explicit clarification of what the parties understand.

There are considerable variations in treaty language, resulting from the negotiation of each individual treaty, mostly based on a model agreement used from time to time by the parties. Some formulations may be less common. Some treaties make reference to "all matters" covered by the IIA (see box 22). Others clarify that MFN treatment applies to the whole provisions of the IIA (see box 23). The latter has been the classic approach followed by the United Kingdom, although some of its recent treaties do not include said formula: specifically the BITs concluded with Viet Nam (2002) and Mexico (2006). Last but not least, some treaties link MFN treatment with the Fair and Equitable Treatment obligation (see box 24)

Box 21. BIPA Indian model text (2003)

Article 4
National Treatment and Most-Favoured-Nation Treatment

(1) Each Contracting Party shall accord to investments of investors of the other Contracting Party, treatment which shall not be less favourable than that accorded either to investments of its own or investments of investors of any third State.

(2) In addition, each Contracting Party shall accord to investors of the other Contracting Party, including in respect of returns on their investments, treatment which shall not be less favourable than that accorded to investors of any third State. [...]

Box 22. Argentina-Spain BIT (1991)

Article 4
Treatment
[...]

*2. **In all matters subject to this Agreement**, this treatment shall be no less favourable than that extended by each Party to the investments made in its territory by investors of a third country.* [unofficial translation]

The examples referred to above illustrate the diversity of approaches and formulations of an MFN treatment clause in IIAs. It is worth noting in this context that very few BITs – with the notable exception of the UK BITs – tackle the issue of whether MFN treatment should apply to encompass ISDS provisions. As will be shown in the following section, specific language in the treaty may not prevent a broad interpretation of MFN treatment clauses by an arbitral tribunal. It is therefore advisable for negotiators to craft the MFN treatment clause very carefully, not only as far as its subject matter and substantive scope is concerned. It is also important to pay attention to possible broad or unexpected interpretations. If the parties to an IIA wish to give the clause more certainty and clarity, they would have to introduce specific language aimed at targeting the intended outcome.

Box 23. El Salvador-United Kingdom BIT (1999)

Article 3
National Treatment and Most-favoured-nation Provisions

[...]

3. *For the avoidance of doubt it is confirmed that the treatment provided for in paragraphs (1) and (2) above shall apply to the provisions of Articles 1 to 11* [investor-State disputes] *of this Agreement.*

Box 24. Morocco-Senegal BIT (2006)

Article 3

(1) *Each Contracting Party shall guarantee on its territory to investments of the other Contracting Party fair and equitable treatment, which is no less favorable than that accorded to investments of its own investors or to investments of the most favored nation whichever is more favorable.* [unofficial translation]

Before looking into the interpretation given to MFN treatment in IIAs in the following sections, it should be stressed that careful crafting of the provisions, in line with policy objectives and specific wording, are crucial in order to make the intention of the parties clear and the interpretation predictable.

B. MFN and the importing of substantive protection provisions from other IIAs

This section will review arbitral awards that have interpreted and applied MFN treatment clauses. As mentioned above, treaty practice has focused on the substantive application of MFN to investment liberalization, i.e. establishment and operational conditions. With the first NAFTA cases, arbitral tribunals have started looking into the application of MFN treatment to import better substantive protection standards claimed by investors.

1. Importing "more favourable" substantive protection standards

In *AAPL v. Republic of Sri Lanka*,[2] the first claim under a BIT, the claimant sought to benefit from an allegedly broader liability standard contained in a third treaty. The MFN claim was rejected on the ground that the claimant had failed to show that the other BIT did in fact offer more favourable treatment. However, the Tribunal did not rule out such an argument in principle.

In *ADF v. United States*,[3] the claimant sought to benefit from an allegedly broader fair and equitable treatment provision contained in third party BITs concluded by the United States with Albania and Estonia. The objective was to circumvent the more restrictive interpretation given to the fair and equitable treatment provision of NAFTA (Article 1105) by the NAFTA Free Trade Commission (FTC) in 2001. The FTC had expressly referred to the customary international law minimum standard of treatment. The tribunal rejected the investor's claim as it assumed "the validity of its own reading of the relevant clauses of the treaties with Albania and Estonia". In its view, the investor did not document the existence, in current international law, of such "autonomous standards", or assuming their hypothetical existence, that "United States measures were reasonably characterized as in breach of such standards".[4] It is worth noting that there is a series of ongoing cases and notices of intent under NAFTA (1992) in which the claimants have raised similar arguments. The aim is to lower the threshold of Article 1105 by pointing to third party BITs concluded by the Unites States and Canada, which allegedly contain "free-standing" fair and equitable treatment provisions. Third treaties here are older versions of the United States and Canadian BITs, as opposed to the current United States and Canadian model BITs which conform to the interpretation given to the fair and equitable treatment standard by the FTC in 2001.

Some awards have used provisions in third party treaties to clarify the meaning of words used in the basic treaty. For example, in *CME v. Czech Republic* the tribunal interpreted the phrase "just compensation" in the expropriation clause in the Czech Republic-Netherlands BIT to mean the same as the "fair market value" criterion used in the Czech Republic-United States BIT (1991).[5]

2. Importing protection provisions which are absent in the basic treaty

In *MTD v. Chile*,[6] the claimant used the MFN clause in the Chile-Malaysia BIT (1992) to argue that more favourable substantive provisions contained in third treaties should apply. The claimants had been denied the required planning licences to develop an investment in property development, although they had received authorization by the Chilean investment authority at the central level. Among other arguments, the claimant invoked Articles 3(1) of the Chile-Denmark BIT (1993) and 3(3-4) of the Chile-Croatia BIT (1994), requiring the granting of "necessary permits" subsequent to approval and the fulfilment of contractual obligations. The tribunal concluded that including such provisions as part of the protection "was in consonance" with the purpose of the basic BIT to "protect and create more favourable investments". It also held that exclusions in the MFN clause relate to tax treatment and regional cooperation, hence "*contrario sensu*" other subject matters that are not specifically excluded from the operation of the MFN clause could be construed to be part of the fair and equitable treatment.[7] It is worth noting here that under the basic BIT, FET was linked to MFN treatment.

The tribunal in *Bayindir v. Pakistan*[8] found that the obligation to grant FET could be read into the basic treaty, the Pakistan-Turkey BIT (1995), even though this treaty did not contain an FET clause. The tribunal noted that Pakistan did not dispute the claimant's assertion that it had concluded several BITs with other countries containing an "explicit fair and equitable treatment clause" and went on to conclude, without further elaboration, that under the circumstances and for the purposes of assessing jurisdiction "*prima facie,* Pakistan was bound to treat investments of Turkish nationals fairly and equitably".[9] It should be noted that this was a decision on jurisdiction and that the finding was only a *prima facie* finding. The tribunal nevertheless reaffirmed the decision on jurisdiction in this regard and held that the fair and equitable treatment standard could be read into the Pakistan-Turkey BIT on the basis of the wording of the MFN clause and because the preamble of the treaty referred to the fair and equitable standard as well. The tribunal went on to consider which of the other BITs signed by Pakistan and containing a fair and equitable treatment clause should constitute the third party treaty. It concluded that this should be the Pakistan-Switzerland treaty (1995) on the ground that it was concluded later in time (i.e. in July rather than in March 1995).[10]

3. **Altering scope of the treaty: *ratione temporis* and *ratione materiae***

In *TECMED v. Mexico*,[11] the claimant sought a retroactive application of its claim by requesting the application of a more favourable *ratione temporis* clause of the Australia-Mexico BIT. The purpose was to include within the claim certain acts that occurred prior to the entry into force of the basic treaty, the Mexico-Spain BIT (2006), deemed as "preparatory for subsequent conduct". The tribunal, rejecting the request, concluded as follows:

> "...*matters relating to the application over time of the Agreement, which involve more the time dimension of application of its substantive provisions rather than matters of procedure or jurisdiction, due to their significance and importance, go **to the core of matters that must be deemed to be specifically negotiated by the Contracting Parties.** These are determining factors for their acceptance of the Agreement, as they are directly linked to the identification of the substantive protection regime applicable to the foreign investor and, particularly, to the general (national or international) legal context within which such regime operates, as well as to the access of the foreign investor to the substantive provisions of such regime. **Their application cannot** therefore be impaired by the principle contained in the most favored nation clause.*" [12]
> [emphasis added]

In addition to matters relating to temporal scope, it remains unclear which other substantive provisions, if any, could qualify as "core matters" under this criteria. It should be noted in this context that the tribunal in this case implied that some provisions are specifically negotiated whereas others are not.

Similarly in *MCI v. Ecuador*,[13] the tribunal was asked by the claimant to modify the temporal application of the basic BIT to include facts that took place prior to its entry into force. The claimant asked the tribunal to look at the Argentina-Ecuador BIT (1994) as the third party BIT. The tribunal followed the respondent's main objections, based strongly on the *Tecmed v. Mexico* decision, with respect to the non-retroactivity of the BIT.

In *Société Generale v. Dominican Republic*,[14] the tribunal dealt with a *ratione materiae* issue. The respondent argued that the tribunal had no jurisdiction given the absence of a qualifying investment under the basic treaty, the Dominican Republic-France BIT (1999). The claimant contented that although it did not meet the investment definition as contained in the Dominican Republic-France BIT (1999), it met the investment definition as contained in the DR-CAFTA (2004). The tribunal found that the investor had made an investment under the basic treaty, but in any case rejected the proposed alternative:

> "*Each treaty defines what it considers a protected investment and who is entitled to that protection, and definitions can change from treaty to treaty. In this situation, resort to the specific text of the MFN clause is unnecessary because it applies only to the treatment accorded to such defined investment, but not to the definition of 'investment' itself.*"[15]

In their reasoning, the arbitrators analysed a basic legal notion: in order to resort to the MFN treatment clause, the basic treaty has to be validly invoked. In other words, first comes the application of the treaty itself, through the scope and definition clauses, and only after this first step, the beneficiary of the MFN clause (the investor) may invoke the clause to seek the better substantive content.

4. Eliminating provisions of the basic treaty

Other cases have dealt with a different scenario where the claimant seeks to eliminate a non-beneficial provision of the basic treaty on grounds that it is not contained in a third party treaty. The absence of such a clause would, in the claimant's view, make the conditions of the third party treaty more favourable. For example in *CMS v. Argentina*[16] the claimant sought to avoid the application of the emergency exception clause contained in the basic treaty between the United States and Argentina. The Tribunal was not convinced that this clause had any role to play in the case and concluded that:

> "*Thus, had other Article XI type clauses envisioned in those treaties a treatment more favorable to the investor, the argument about the operation of the MFNC might have been made. However, the mere absence of such provision in other treaties does not lend support to this argument, which would in any event fail under the ejusdem generis rule, as rightly argued by the Respondent.*" [17]

It should be noted that this decision suggests that the absence of a provision in a third treaty cannot be the basis for excluding a provision contained in the basic treaty by invoking an MFN provision.

5. Comparing treatment: treatment "in like circumstances", identifying better treatment

Two recent arbitral awards have considered the issue of "like circumstances" in the context of MFN treatment. In *Parkerings v. Lithuania*[18] the tribunal held that a comparison was necessary with an investor in like circumstances. In the case where foreign investors were competing for the same public procurement project the tribunal compared not only two investors in the same economic sector but also the characteristics of their respective project proposals. Similarly, in *Bayindir v. Pakistan* (merits) the tribunal established that the similarity and hence the comparability between the foreign investors had to be examined at the level of the contractual terms and circumstances. It is worth noting here that in these two cases the underlying MFN clause does not make a reference to "like circumstances" or any similar wording. This would suggest that, as mentioned earlier, a requirement to compare comparable investors/investments constitutes an implicit element of the functioning of an MFN treatment clause and does not need to be specified.

The comparison test has in practice worked differently depending on what claimants were seeking from the MFN clause. When claimants were seeking better treatment, whether material or effective, such as in the cases referred to above, tribunals have compared treatment amongst two foreign investors who are in identical circumstances. But when claimants have invoked the MFN treatment clause in order to attract the benefits of ISDS or substantive protection provisions from third treaties, tribunals have been satisfied with the mere fact that the claimant qualifies as an "investor" under the basic treaty and have not gone into actually comparing the investor with another foreign investor from a third country.

In *Parkerings v. Lithuania*, the claimant argued that the host State did not provide the same standard of treatment contrary to what is required by the MFN clause, alleging that a Dutch company was selected as the successful tenderer and was awarded the contract for the construction of the project whereas the claimant's (a Norwegian company) offer had been rejected. The tribunal recalled that the MFN treatment and NT were by essence very similar. It held that they have similar conditions of application and basically afford indirect advantages to their beneficiaries, namely a treatment no less favourable than the one granted to third parties. It then elaborated on the basis of comparison that had to be met:

> *"Discrimination is to be ascertained by looking at the circumstances of the individual cases. Discrimination involves either issues of law, such as legislation affording different treatments in function of citizenship, or issues of fact where a State unduly treats differently investors who are in similar circumstances. […] However, to violate international law, discrimination must be unreasonable or lacking proportionality, for instance, it must be inapposite or excessive to achieve an*

otherwise legitimate objective of the State. An objective justification may justify differentiated treatments of similar cases. It would be necessary, in each case, to evaluate the exact circumstances and the context.

The essential condition of the violation of a MFN clause is the existence of a different treatment accorded to another foreign investor in a similar situation. Therefore, a comparison is necessary with an investor in like circumstances. The notion of like circumstances has been broadly analysed by Tribunals."[19]

The tribunal used the test of the "same economic or business sector" and further considered any policy or purpose behind the measure that could justify a difference in treatment. Even though the relevant comparators were engaged in similar activities (they were competitors for the same project), the tribunal concluded that the relevant investors were in different circumstances, in particular because their offers and proposed projects had different characteristics.

"... despite similarities in objective and venue, the Tribunal has concluded, on balance, that the differences of size of Pinus Proprius and BP's projects, as well as the significant extension of the latter into the Old Town near the Cathedral area, are important enough to determine that the two investors were not in like circumstances...Thus the City of Vilnius did have legitimate grounds to distinguish between the two projects. Indeed, the refusal by the Municipality of Vilnius to authorize BP's project in Gedimino was justified by various concerns, especially in terms of historical and archaeological preservation and environmental protection."[20]

In *Bayindir v. Pakistan* the claimant alleged that it was expelled both to save costs and for reasons of local favouritism, considering in particular that far more favourable timetables had been accorded to Pakistani nationals associated with foreign contractors and that these other contractors had not been expelled even though they were far more behind in the schedule of completion. As noted in the decision on jurisdiction, the tribunal recalled that the MFN treatment and NT were not limited to regulatory conduct, but also to the manner in which States conclude an investment contract and/or exercise their rights there under. The first step for the tribunal was to determine whether the investor was in a "similar situation" to that of other investors of other nationalities and, if that requirement had been met, inquire if the investor had been granted less favourable treatment. As to the first point, the tribunal established that the similarity had to be examined at the level of the contractual terms and circumstances, but found itself in no position to proceed to any meaningful comparison given the absence of data on the terms and the performance of the different contracts involved. Therefore, it concluded that the arguments were clearly insufficient to substantiate a violation of the MFN treatment provision.

C. MFN and the importing of procedural provisions from other IIAs

The applicability of the MFN treatment clause to ISDS provisions in IIAs has generated numerous arbitral decisions, where jurisdiction of the arbitral tribunal has been challenged by the respondent State. Two categories of cases can be distinguished. In a first set of cases, claimants have invoked the MFN treatment clause to override a procedural requirement that constitutes a condition for the submission of a claim to international arbitration. This has led to a series of cases against Argentina because a number of BITs concluded by Argentina contain a mandatory 18-months waiting period during which claims should be brought before domestic courts (local remedies) before they can be brought to international arbitration. A first significant case was *Maffezini* v. *Spain*,[21] but all the subsequent cases have involved Argentina as the respondent

State. The MFN clause has been invoked to sidestep or circumvent the 18 months local remedies requirement on the ground that third party BITs concluded by the host State (Argentina) do not contain it. The defendant State has argued that the mandatory waiting period was a condition that had to be met for a claim to be brought before an arbitral tribunal and that said arbitral tribunal would not have jurisdiction of the case, lest this condition had been exhausted. The arguments invoked by both parties to these cases will be called "admissibility" requirements.

Under the second category of cases, claimants have attempted to extend via MFN the jurisdictional threshold, i.e. the scope of the mandate of the arbitral tribunal beyond that specifically set forth in the basic treaty This use of the MFN clause would give the arbitral tribunal jurisdiction to hear issues or disputes that the basic treaty does not contemplate or expressly excludes. Cases here have involved a request to bring contractual claims before a treaty based arbitration panel and a number of requests to extend jurisdiction of arbitral tribunals beyond assessing the amount of compensation subsequent to expropriation. This second category of cases will be looked at under the heading of "scope of jurisdiction" requirements.

1. "Admissibility" requirements

In *Maffezzini* v. *Spain* the tribunal held that the MFN treatment clause in the Argentina-Spain BIT (1991) could be used by the claimant to circumvent or dispense with an 18-month waiting period before recourse to international arbitration was available. The argument used by the claimant was that the third treaty concluded between Spain and Chile did not contain such a requirement and that the ISDS clause in this third treaty was therefore less restrictive. It could then be imported using the MFN clause contained in the basic treaty. Relying strongly on the *Ambiatelos* decision, the tribunal found that even though the MFN clause did not expressly refer to dispute settlement "there were good reasons to conclude that dispute settlement arrangements were inextricably related to the protection of foreign investors". It further elaborated as follows:

> "... it can be concluded that if a third-party treaty contains provisions for the settlement of disputes that are more favorable to the protection of the investor's rights and interests than those in the basic treaty, such provisions may be extended to the beneficiary of the most favored nation clause as they are fully compatible with the ejusdem generis principle. Of course, the third-party treaty has to relate to the same subject matter as the basic treaty, be it the protection of foreign investments or the promotion of trade, since the dispute settlement provisions will operate in the context of these matters; otherwise there would be a contravention of that principle. This operation of the most favored nation clause does, however, have some important limits arising from public policy considerations that will be discussed further below."[22]

The tribunal examined Spain's negotiation practice, which indicated "Spain's preference to allow for arbitration, following a six-months effort to reach a friendly settlement". In addition, the broad wording of the MFN treatment clause referring to "all matters" was only to be found in the treaty concluded between Spain and Argentina but not in any other of the BITs concluded by Spain.

However, the tribunal recognized some "important limits that ought to be kept in mind" and put certain limits to the MFN clause in the following terms:

> "... As a matter of principle, the beneficiary of the clause should not be able to override public policy considerations that the contracting parties might have envisaged as fundamental conditions for their acceptance of the agreement in question, particularly if the beneficiary is a private investor, as will often be the case. The scope of the clause might thus be narrower

than it appears at first sight.

It is clear, in any event, that a distinction has to be made between the legitimate extension of rights and benefits by means of the operation of the clause, on the one hand, and disruptive treaty-shopping that would play havoc with the policy objectives of underlying specific treaty provisions, on the other hand." [23]

The tribunal goes on and gives examples of provisions that could not be overridden by the MFN clause as the effect would be to *"upset the finality of arrangements that many countries deem important as a matter of public policy"* were: (i) the agreement to arbitrate on the condition to exhaust local remedies, (ii) the fork in the road rule, (iii) the establishment of a particular forum such as the ICSID, and (iv) the agreement to arbitrate under a highly institutionalized system of arbitration such as the NAFTA (1992) or similar arrangements.

This decision started an intense debate that continues to date as to whether MFN treatment includes access to international arbitration as contained in the ISDS provisions of respective agreements.

The same issue arose in *Siemens v. Argentina.*[24] Here the tribunal rejected the respondent's view that MFN treatment only covers "treatment of transactions of a commercial and economic nature in relation to exploitation and management of investments" or "competitiveness of the investments." Using a similar reasoning than that of *Maffezini v. Spain* it concluded that:

"... the Treaty itself [the Argentine-Germany BIT], *together with so many other treaties of investment protection, had as a distinctive feature special dispute settlement mechanisms not normally open to investors. Access to these mechanisms is part of the protection afforded under the Treaty. It is part of the*

treatment of foreign investors and investments and of the advantages accessible through a MFN clause."[25]

The tribunal held that "*the purpose of the MFN clause is to eliminate the effect of specially negotiated provisions unless they have been excepted*".[26] This statement can be considered as overly broad. The tribunal further rejected an argument raised by the respondent, that if the investor was to import advantageous aspects of a third treaty it had to import the disadvantageous aspects as well (although it recognized the merit in the proposition as treaties are negotiated "as a package" and the disadvantages may constitute a trade-off for the advantages):

"[…] *Even if the MFN clause is of a general nature, its application will be related only to the benefits that the treaty of reference may grant and to the extent that benefits are perceived to be such.*"[27]

In *Gas Natural v. Argentina,* after finding that ISDS provisions constitute part of the package of protection granted to foreign investors and a "significant incentive" given by host States, the tribunal held that "[…] *Unless it appears clearly that the state parties to a BIT or the parties to a particular investment agreement settled on a different method for resolution of disputes that may arise, most-favored-nation provisions in BITs should be understood to be applicable to dispute settlement*".[28] *Suez v. Argentina* took a similar approach when affirming that "[…] *From the point of view of the promotion and protection of investments, the stated purpose of the Argentina-Spain BIT, dispute settlement is as important as other matters governed by the BIT and is an integral part of the investment protection regime that two sovereign states, Argentina and Spain, had agreed upon*".[29] The tribunal also focused on the MFN clause wording referring to "all matters" as well as its list of exceptions none of which includes ISDS. The tribunals in *Cammuzi v. Argentina,*[30] *National Grid v. Argentina*[31] and *AWG v. Argentina*[32] came to similar conclusions.

Some of the cases cited above that followed *Maffezini v. Spain* were based on treaties with different wordings but came to the same conclusion: the 18-months waiting period was disregarded and the tribunal had jurisdiction. The main argument seems to be that ISDS provisions form an integral part of the protection of foreign investors (*Maffezini, Suez, AWG Group, National Grid*). Consequently "*access to these* [procedural] *mechanisms is part of the protection afforded under the treaty*" (*Siemens v. Argentina,* para. 102) and access to international arbitration constitutes "*a crucial element – indeed perhaps the most crucial element*" in BITs (*Gas Natural v. Argentina,* para. 29). These arguments draw on the object and purpose of the underlying IIA, sometimes understood from the preamble. Other arguments include the wording and grammatical construction of the MFN clause, including the principle of "*expressio unis et exclusio*"[33] and Argentina's negotiation practice as to the inclusion of the 18-months requirement.

Arbitral tribunals in these cases did not see an MFN clause as having an unlimited reach nonetheless. They followed the reasoning of the tribunal in *Maffezini v. Spain* and listed a series of limitations to the operation of MFN provisions. As referred above, certain public policy limitations, taken by the parties to the agreement, were taken into account.[34] Moreover, a distinction was made between "the legitimate extension of rights and benefits by means of the operation of the clause, on the one hand, and disruptive treaty shopping that would play havoc with the policy objectives of underlying specific treaty provisions, on the other hand."[35] In similar terms the *Siemens v. Argentina* tribunal established "that the beneficiary of the MFN clause may not override public policy considerations judged by the parties to a treaty essential to their agreement".[36] The tribunal in *Gas Natural v. Argentina* rejected the argument that the 18-months waiting period was a "public policy rule"[37] whereas the tribunal in *National Grid v. Argentina* accepted that some claimants had tried to use the MFN clause "beyond reasonable limits".[38]

Yet in a more recent case, this approach was rejected by an arbitral tribunal dealing with the local remedies requirement in Argentine BITs. In *Wintershall v. Argentina,*[39] the claimant sought to override the requirement arguing that it did not involve jurisdiction, consent or any "public policy" provision. It also raised the arguments that had been used by the previous tribunals dealing with the same issue.

However, the tribunal then went on to qualify this argument that the issue at stake did not relate to consent or jurisdiction as "plainly erroneous". In doing so it gave particular weight to the "consent" as the founding principle upon which jurisdiction is formed:

> *"Besides, it is a general principle of international law that international courts and tribunals can exercise jurisdiction over a State only with its consent. The principle is often described as a corollary to the sovereignty and independence of the State. A presumed consent is not regarded as sufficient, because any restriction upon the independence of a State (not agreed to) cannot be presumed by courts ..."*40

The tribunal considered that the "timing rule" (the 18-months waiting period) rule constituted "part and parcel of Argentina's integrated offer for ICSID arbitration" which should be "accepted by the investor on the same terms". The tribunal also based its decision on an analysis of the MFN clause wording and found that the "treatment" to which it extended did not include dispute settlement. The tribunal concluded as follows:

> *"... ordinarily and without more, the prospect of an investor selecting at will from an assorted variety of options provided in other treaties negotiated with other parties under different circumstances, dislodges the dispute resolution provision in the basic treaty itself – unless of course the MFN clause in the basic treaty clearly and unambiguously indicates that it should be so interpreted: which is not so in the present case."*[41]

Criticizing *Siemens* the tribunal was of the opinion that:

"[...] *Adding words to a treaty on the basis of presumed intention must be avoided. It is an exercise that has been characterized as an interpretation that "tends to* create *meaning rather than to* discover *it."* [42]

The tribunal added that:

"Even words like 'all matters relating to [...]' in an MFN clause may not be sufficient to extend such clause to the dispute resolution provisions of the BIT." [43]

It should be mentioned that, independently of the analysis that tribunals make of the nature and scope of the consent given under ISDS clauses, the actual wording used in an MFN treatment clause matters and a broad wording can not be simply discarded by an arbitral tribunal.

2. "Jurisdictional" requirements

Under this second category, a number of cases have rejected the *Maffezini v. Spain* approach on grounds that an MFN treatment clause cannot be used to upset or circumvent the jurisdictional requirements of the basic BIT. Cases following this approach include *Salini, Plama, Telenor* and *Berschader*. In these cases, tribunals have expressed their doubt that the Contracting Parties could reasonably have intended that jurisdiction was to be formed through an incorporation by reference, unless such intent had been explicitly reflected in the relevant ISDS provisions of the basic BIT.

In *Salini v. Jordan*[44] the investor relied upon the MFN treatment clause in order to bring contractual claims before an ICSID tribunal given that the basic treaty, the Italy-Jordan BIT (2001), provides that any dispute related to an investment contract is to be settled under its terms. While reviewing the early cases relating to the issue, the tribunal dismissed any analogy with *Ambiatelos*. The tribunal was also critical of *Maffezini v. Spain* observing that the reasoning *"may in practice prove difficult to apply, thereby adding more uncertainties to the risk of 'treaty shopping'."*[45] The tribunal further observed that the MFN clause did not include any provision extending its scope of application to ISDS:

> *"... the Claimants have submitted nothing from which it might be established that the common intention of the Parties was to have the most-favored-nation clause apply to dispute settlement. Quite on the contrary, the intention as expressed in Article 9(2) of the BIT was to exclude from ICSID jurisdiction contractual disputes between an investor and an entity of a State Party in order that such disputes might be settled in accordance with the procedures set forth in the investment agreements. Lastly, the Claimants had not cited any practice in Jordan or Italy in support of their claims."*[46]

In *Plama v. Bulgaria*,[47] the claimant sought to broaden the scope of jurisdiction of the basic BIT, confined in the text to controversies related to compensation in case of an expropriation. The claimant was hoping to achieve this by referring to a third BIT containing a broader ISDS clause open to other types of claims. However, the tribunal did not accept the arguments advanced by the claimant, although these arguments had been decisive in those cases dealing with the 18-months requirement (see above). The tribunal also looked into the history of BITs concluded by Bulgaria and took into account the fact that Bulgaria used to negotiate restrictive BITs during the communist regime and that the negotiations between Bulgaria and Cyprus seeking to revise their BIT in 1998 were inconclusive on this particular issue of the scope of the ISDS provision.

The tribunal relied on an established principle, "both in domestic and international law", that an agreement to arbitrate should be "clear and unambiguous", and consequently stated that the parties' clear and unambiguous intention could not be identified if the agreement to arbitrate was to be reached through incorporation by reference.

Moreover, the tribunal emphasized the need for an objective test of less favourable treatment:

"Moreover, the doubt as to the relevance of the MFN clause in one BIT to the incorporation of dispute resolution provisions in other agreements is compounded by the difficulty of applying an objective test to the issue of what is more favorable. The Claimant argues that it is obviously more favorable for the investor to have a choice among different dispute resolution mechanisms, and to have the entire dispute resolved by arbitration as provided in the Bulgaria-Finland BIT, than to be confined to ad hoc arbitration limited to the quantum of compensation for expropriation. The Tribunal is inclined to agree with the Claimant that in this particular case, a choice is better than no choice. But what if one BIT provides for UNCITRAL arbitration and another provides for ICSID? Which is more favorable?" [48]

It also placed great importance on the radical effects sought by the claimant. It made reference to the risks of an uncontained "treaty shopping":

"… It is one thing to add to the treatment provided in one treaty more favorable treatment provided elsewhere. It is quite another thing to replace a procedure specifically negotiated by parties with an entirely different mechanism." [49]

"… When concluding a multilateral or bilateral investment treaty with specific dispute resolution provisions, states cannot be expected to leave those provisions to future (partial)

replacement by different dispute resolution provisions through the operation of an MFN provision, unless the States have explicitly agreed...The present Tribunal fails to see how harmonization of dispute settlement provisions can be achieved by reliance on the MFN provision. Rather, the "basket of treatment" and 'self-adaptation of an MFN provision' in relation to dispute settlement provisions (as alleged by the Claimant) has as effect that an investor has the option to pick and choose provisions from the various BITs. If that were true, a host state which has not specifically agreed thereto can be confronted with a large number of permutations of dispute settlement provisions from the various BITs which it has concluded. Such a chaotic situation—actually counterproductive to harmonization—cannot be the presumed intent of Contracting Parties."[50]

After having reviewed previous relevant cases (with some critics to both *Maffezini v. Spain* and *Siemens v. Argentina*) it concluded as follows:

"... an MFN provision in a basic treaty does not incorporate by reference dispute settlement provisions in whole or in part set forth in another treaty, unless the MFN provision in the basic treaty leaves no doubt that the Contracting Parties intended to incorporate them." [51]

In *Telenor v. Hungary,*[52] as in *Plama v. Bulgaria,* the question arose whether the MFN clause could be used to extend claims beyond those of compensation for expropriation. Having rejected the claim, the tribunal *"wholeheartedly"* endorsed the statement of principle made by the tribunal in *Plama v. Bulgaria* based on *"four compelling reasons"*:

The first and fourth reasons related to an interpretative exercise:

"... In the absence of language or context to suggest the contrary, the ordinary meaning of 'investments shall be

accorded treatment no less favourable than that accorded to investments made by investors of any third State' is that the investor's substantive rights in respect of the investments are to be treated no less favourably than under a BIT between the host State and a third State, and there is no warrant for construing the above phrase as importing procedural rights as well. It is one thing to stipulate that the investor is to have the benefit of MFN investment treatment but quite another to use an MFN clause in a BIT to bypass a limitation in the very same BIT when the parties have not chosen language in the MFN clause showing an intention to do this, as has been done in some BITs.

[...] in the view of this Tribunal its task is to interpret the BIT and for that purpose to apply ordinary canons of interpretation, not to displace, by reference to general policy considerations concerning investor protection, the dispute resolution mechanism specifically negotiated by the parties."[53]

The second and third reasons related to the risks of "treaty shopping", uncertainty and unpredictability (which could not be reasonably deemed the intention of the parties):

"[...] the effect of the wide interpretation of the MFN clause is to expose the host State to treaty-shopping by the investor among an indeterminate number of treaties to find a dispute resolution clause wide enough to cover a dispute that would fall outside the dispute resolution clause in the base treaty, and even then there would be questions as to whether the investor could select those elements of the wider dispute resolution that were apt for its purpose and discard those that were not.

[...] the wide interpretation also generates both uncertainty and instability in that at one moment the limitation in the basic BIT is operative and at the next moment it is overridden by a wider

dispute resolution clause in a new BIT entered into by the host State."[54]

A similar result was reached in *Berschader v. Russian Federation*.[55] Here the tribunal agreed with the reasoning contained in the *Palma v. Bulgaria* case in the sense that an "agreement to arbitrate should not be reached by incorporation by reference".

"[…] *Thus, while it may be true that no general principle exists, according to which arbitration agreements should be construed restrictively, particular care should nevertheless be exercised in ascertaining the intentions of the parties with regard to an arbitration agreement which is to be reached by incorporation by reference in an MFN clause.*"[56]

At the end the tribunal disagreed with the reasoning held by another arbitral tribunal in the *Gas Natural v. Argentina* award:

"*The tribunal in the Gas Natural case suggested that as a matter of principle MFN provisions in BITs should be understood to be applicable to dispute settlement provisions unless it appears clearly that the parties intended otherwise. For the reasons developed above, it should be evident that this Tribunal cannot accept that standpoint. Instead, the present Tribunal will apply the principle that an MFN provision in a BIT will only incorporate by reference an arbitration clause from another BIT where the terms of the original BIT clearly and unambiguously so provide or where it can otherwise be clearly inferred that this was the intention of the contracting parties.*"[57]

The tribunal rejected the argument that access to arbitration is in fact such an important form of investment protection that not extending the MFN provisions to arbitration clauses would run counter to the overriding object and purpose of a BIT (the critical argument in the series of cases against Argentina dealing with the

18-months requirement). It saw it as merely generic and of little or no guidance as to determine the intention of the parties to the treaty.

Finally, in *Tza Yap Shum v. Peru*[58], the arbitral tribunal looked into the MFN provision of the China-Peru BIT (1994). Following the traditional treaties concluded by China this agreement was also limited to claims for compensation in case of expropriation. The tribunal did not consider that the "treatment" referred to in the MFN clause was limited to substantial commercial matters nor did it find evidence that the parties had the intention to attribute a specific meaning to it. It recognized that *"when a nation includes one or more MFN provisions in a treaty, it does it purposefully in order to recognize that it is according investors of the other signatory State of the treaty in question [...] more favourable treatment and protection accorded under future treaties"*[unofficial translation] although recognizing that *"each MFN clause is a world in itself, which demands an individualized interpretation to determine its scope of application"* [unofficial translation].[59] At the end, however, the tribunal gave weight to the specific terms of the dispute resolution clause:

> "[...] *the Tribunal hereby determines that the specific wording of Article 8(3) should prevail over the general wording of the MFN clause in Article 3 and Claimant's arguments on the contrary must be dismissed.*" [unofficial translation][60]

It's worth noting that the conclusion was taken given the specific wording of the arbitration clause of the basic BIT, which allowed to expand the jurisdiction beyond expropriation cases only "if the parties so agree".[61]

A certain trend of arbitration tribunals rejecting the establishment of jurisdiction by incorporation by reference through an MFN treatment clause was challenged by the decision in *RosInvestCo v. Russian Federation*,[62] which accepted to extend the scope of jurisdiction through an MFN clause. In doing so, the tribunal stated this *"was a normal result of the application of the MFN clause"*.[63] Although the defending State had recalled that *"every single tribunal that has considered the question of expanding international tribunals' jurisdiction on the basis of a most-favoured-nation clause has rejected the Claimant's position [...]"*.

After recognizing that arbitration forms a *"highly relevant part of the corresponding protection for the investor"* (in para 130), the tribunal concluded that:

> *"[...] While indeed the application of the MFN clause of Article 3 widens the scope of Article 8 [dispute settlement] and thus is in conflict to its limitation, this is a normal result of the application of MFN clauses, the very character and intention of which is that protection not accepted in one treaty is widened by transferring the protection accorded in another treaty."*[64]

For the tribunal, making a difference between "substantive" and "procedural" provisions of the treaty was irrelevant:

> *"If this effect is generally accepted in the context of substantive protection, the Tribunal sees no reason not to accept it in the context of procedural clauses such as arbitration clauses. Quite the contrary, it could be argued that, if it applies to substantive protection, then it should apply even more to 'only' procedural protection. However, the Tribunal feels that this latter argument cannot be considered as decisive, but that rather, as argued further above, an arbitration clause, at least in the context of expropriation, is of the same protective value as any substantive protection afforded by applicable provisions such as Article 5 of the BIT."*[65]

More recently, in *Renta v. Russian Federation*,[66] the tribunal had to look again into the MFN clause and whether it could be used to broaden the scope of jurisdiction beyond expropriation claims. For the tribunal, the fundamental issue was to determine whether the access to arbitration formed part and parcel of the treatment owed to a foreign investor through an MFN treatment clause.

> "... *It is not convincing for a State to argue in general terms that it accepted a particular system of arbitration with respect to nationals of one country but did not so consent with respect to nationals of another. The extension of commitments is the very nature of the MFN clause. Drafters wishing to do so would have little difficulty in defining restrictions that would go further than the ejusdem generis constraint...*"[67]

The tribunal rejected a dichotomy of "primary" and "secondary" rules and held that there was no authority for the proposition that MFN is limited to "primary" obligations. It also held that access to international arbitration had been a fundamental and constant condition for investment protection and therefore a powerful factor in considering the object and purpose of BITs. It also rejected the "invidious" proposition, as some commentators have called it, to assume that investment tribunals were superior to domestic courts and that therefore investors seeking to have their claim assessed by a neutral international forum was based on a rational concern. The tribunal asserted that there was no textual basis or legal rule to say that treatment does not encompass the host State's acceptance of international arbitration.

Examining these arguments lead to a decision by the tribunal in favour of the investor. However, the tribunal noted that the wording of the MFN clause was not phrased in generic terms but only covered "treatment referred to in paragraph 1 above", that is, "fair and equitable treatment". The discussion then turned to the question whether dispute settlement was an inherent part of the "fair and equitable treatment" standard. After a detailed grammatical analysis, the conclusion was in negative terms as follows:

"The conclusion must be that the specific MFN promise contained in Article (5)2 of the [Spain-Russia] *BIT cannot be read to enlarge the competence of the present Tribunal. This conclusion… is that of a majority of the tribunal. The separate opinion appended hereto is viewed with full respect by the majority. They agree that "more favourable" may in principle include accessibility to international fora. Ultimately however their view is that the terms of the Spanish BIT restrict MFN treatment to the realm of* [fair and Equitable Treatment] *as understood in international law. This in the majority view relates to normative standards and does not extend to either (i) availability of international as opposed to national fora or (ii) "more" rather than "less" arbitration"(as the separate opinion puts it).* "[68]

Accordingly, it can be noted that so far a majority of the tribunals looking into the possible incorporation through an MFN treatment clause of broader ISDS provisions declined jurisdiction to hear claims other than those relating to compensation in the case of expropriation.[69]

* * *

The arguments raised by claimants in recent ISDS cases and the decisions by arbitral tribunals are summarized in table 1 (below). Claimants have invoked the relationship between the availability of ISDS and investment protection as a whole, the overall objectives of investment protection agreements, the negotiating context, the wording of the MFN provision itself and its plain reading under the Vienna Convention to seek modification of the basic treaty by incorporation of provisions from a third treaty. To counter these arguments and preserve the integrity of the basic treaty, defendants have argued that the intent of the parties can be deduced from reasonable interpretation and that there is a need for a clear and unambiguous consent. They also claimed that there is no evidence of "less favourable" treatment enshrined in the basic treaty as opposed to a third treaty. Furthermore, MFN is a core matter of fundamental importance that ought not to be changed: In this context they also pointed to the broader risk of treaty shopping.

Table 1. Summary of MFN claims

EFFECT SOUGHT	CASES	RESULT
Override an 18-months waiting period before local courts	*Maffezini v. Spain, Siemens, Gas Natural, Camuzzi, Suez, National Grid, Wintershall v. Argentina*	*Allowed, except for Wintershall*
Submit disputes beyond the jurisdictional threshold	*Plama v. Bulgaria, Salini v. Jordan, Telenor Mobile v. Hungary, RosInvestCo v. Russia, Berschader v. Russia, Renta 4S v. Russia, Tza Yap Shum v. Peru*	*Denied, except for RosInvestCo*
Benefit from additional substantive content	*Bayindir v. Pakistan, MTD Equity v. Chile*	*Allowed*
Benefit from like provisions perceived as "more favourable"	*AAPL v. Sri Lanka, ADF v. United States*	*Denied*
Alter the BIT's scope of application (ratione temporis or ratione materiae)	*Tecmed v. Mexico, MCI v. Ecuador, Société Generale v. Dominican Republic*	*Denied*
Override a general emergency exception clause	*CMS v. Argentina*	*Denied*
Change the standard of compensation for expropriation	*CME v. Czech Republic*	*Allowed*
Compare treatment amongst two foreign investors	*Bayindir v. Pakistan, Parkerings v. Lithuania*	*No breach found*

Various messages and words of caution can be taken from the two tables:

- A majority of arbitral tribunals has held that an MFN treatment clause can be used to incorporate into the basic treaty a shorter waiting period, such as for example circumventing an 18-months waiting period or applying less stringent admissibility conditions.
- A majority of arbitral tribunals has held that an MFN treatment clause cannot, however, be used to incorporate less stringent or broader jurisdictional requirements, such as broadening the scope of an ISDS provision beyond a dispute relating to the amount of compensation in the case of an expropriation.

- In most of the cases, however, the arbitral tribunal paid particular attention to the wording of the MFN treatment clause in the underlying treaty in order to support their reasoning.

D. A reaction by States entering into investment agreements: narrowing the scope of an MFN clause

The above interpretations of an MFN treatment clause by arbitral tribunals, both in relation to substantive and procedural effects, have generated concerns for negotiators as far as the extent of the commitment of the State is concerned. In particular, the application of MFN to import more favourable ISDS procedure provisions and to broaden the scope of ISDS provision would appear to allow for a rewriting of the BIT in question. It is difficult to assume that negotiating parties actually considered the implications of the MFN clause on ISDS provisions when concluding their agreements. Such claims have only arisen very recently while most BITs were negotiated some years ago. In response some IIAs are introducing clarifications and guidance on the operation of the MFN clause, aimed at avoiding broad arbitral interpretations allowing for procedural provisions in third party treaties to be incorporated by reference into basic treaties.

In the context of negotiation of a Free Trade Agreement of the Americas (FTAA), the investment working group submitted a draft in November 2003 with the following footnote:[70]

"**Note:** One delegation proposes the following footnote to be included in the negotiating history as a reflection of the Parties' shared understanding of the Most-Favored-Nation Article and the *Maffezini* case. This footnote would be deleted in the final text of the Agreement:

"The Parties note the recent decision of the arbitral tribunal in the Maffezini (Arg.) v. Kingdom of Spain, which found an unusually broad most favored nation clause in an Argentina-Spain agreement to encompass international dispute resolution procedures. See Decision on Jurisdiction §§ 38-64 (January 25, 2000), reprinted in 16 ICSID Rev.-F.I.L.J. 212 (2002). By contrast, the Most-Favored-Nation Article of this Agreement is expressly limited in its scope to matters "with respect to the establishment, acquisition, expansion, management, conduct, operation, and sale or other disposition of investments." The Parties share the understanding and intent that this clause does not encompass international dispute resolution mechanisms such as those contained in Section C.2.b (Dispute Settlement between a Party and an Investor of Another Party) of this Chapter, and therefore could not reasonably lead to a conclusion similar to that of the Maffezini case."

This text, later known as the *"Maffezini* Note", was the result of strong disagreement by many States in Latin America to the decision and reasoning of the *Maffezini v Spain* tribunal. The trend to incorporate clarification into IIAs continues as many recent IIAs include a less elaborated but equally clear clarification on the scope of the application of MFN treatment (whether in a footnote, annex or directly as part of the MFN clause) (see box 25).

Box 25. Examples of MFN clauses restricting incorporation by reference

Chile-Colombia FTA (2006)

Annex 9.3
Most-Favoured-Nation Treatment

"The Parties agree that the scope of application of Article 9.3 only covers the matters related to the establishment, acquisition, expansion, administration, conduct, operation, sale or other disposition of investments, and hence, does not apply to procedural issues, including dispute settlement mechanisms such as that contained in Section B of this Chapter."
(unofficial translation)

Other recent examples include the Annex 884.1 of the Canada-Peru FTA (2008) (see box 26) and paragraph 2 of Article 88 of the Japan-Switzerland EPA (2009) (see box 27).

Box 26. Canada-Peru FTA (2008)

Annex 804.1
Most-Favoured-Nation Treatment

For greater clarity, treatment 'with respect to the establishment, acquisition, expansion, management, conduct, operation and sale or other disposition of investments' referred to in paragraphs 1 and 2 of Article 804 does not encompass dispute resolution mechanisms, such as those in Section B, that are provided for in international treaties or trade agreements.

Box 27. Japan-Switzerland EPA (2009)

Article 88
2. It is understood that the treatment referred to in paragraph 1 does not include treatment accorded to investors of a non-Party and their investments by provisions concerning the settlement of investment disputes between a Party and the non-Party that are provided for in other international agreements.

Negotiators and policymakers should therefore also be aware that, as for any other provision of the investment treaty, wording matters and the formulation resulting from the negotiation should make the intention of the parties clear and unambiguous, particularly as far as the MFN treatment provision is concerned. The following section will look in details into various options to ensure clarification of the scope and functioning of the MFN treatment clause and provide guidance to arbitral tribunals as to the underlying policy objectives on the part of the States parties to the treaty.

Notes

[1] By means of the "negative" list, the most common approach, MFN treatment is afforded to all sectors and activities except for those specifically set forth in the list. By means of the "positive" list MFN treatment is afforded only to those sectors and activities specifically set forth in the list, such as the Australia-Thailand FTA (2004).

2 *Asian Agricultural Products Ltd. (AAPL) v. Republic of Sri Lanka, ICSID Case No. ARB/87/3, Final Award, 27 June 1990.*

3 *ADF Group Inc. v. The United States of America, ICSID Case No. ARB(AF)/00/1, Award, 9 January 2003.*

4 Ibid., para. 194.

5 *CME Czech Republic B.V. v. The Czech Republic, UNCITRAL, Final Award, 14 March 2003:* "The determination of compensation under the Treaty between the Netherlands and the Czech Republic on basis of the "fair market value" finds support in the "most-favored-nation provision of Art. 3(5) of the Treaty…" The bilateral treaty between the United States of America and the Czech Republic provides that compensation shall be equivalent to the fair market value of the expropriated investment immediately before the expropriation action was taken. The Czech Republic therefore is obligated to provide no less than "fair market value" to Claimant in respect of its investment, should (in contrast to this Tribunal's opinion) "just compensation" representing the "genuine value" be interpreted to be less than "fair market value" [para. 500].

6 *MTD Equity Sdn. Bhd. & MTD Chile S.A. v. Chile, ICSID Case No. ARB/01/7, Award, 25 May 2004,* para. 104. The Annulment Committee did not overturn the tribunal on this issue: Annulment Proceeding 21 March 2007, para. 64.

7 Ibid., para. 104.

8 *Bayindir Insaat Turizm Ticaret Ve Sanayi AS v. Islamic Republic of Pakistan, ICSID Case No. ARB/03/29, Decision on Jurisdiction, 14 November 2005,* paras. 227–235.

9 Ibid., para. 232.

10 *Bayindir Insaat Turizm Ticaret Ve Sanayi AS v. Islamic Republic of Pakistan, ICSID Case No. ARB/03/29, Award, 27 August 2009,* para. 163-167.

11 *Tecnicas Mediambientales Tecmed S.A. v. the United Mexican States, ICSID Case no. ARB (AF)/00/02, Award, 29 May 2003.*

12 Ibid., para. 69.

[13] *M.C.I. Power Group L.C. and New Urbine, Inc. V. Republic of Ecuador, ICSID Case No. ARB/03/6, Award, 31 July 2007.*

[14] *Société Generale v. The Dominican Republic*, LCAI Case No. UN 7927, Award on Preliminary Objections to Jurisdiction.

[15] Ibid., para. 41.

[16] *CMS Gas Transmission Company v. The Argentine Republic*, ICSID Case No. ARB701/08, Award, 25 April 2005.

[17] Ibid., p. 377.

[18] *Parkerings-Compagniet AS v. Republic of Lithuania*, ICSID Case No. ARB/05/8, Award, 11 September 2007.

[19] Ibid., para. 368-369.

[20] Ibid., para. 396.

[21] *Emilio Agustín Maffezini and The Kingdom of Spain*, ICSID Case No. ARB/97/7, Decision of the tribunal on the objections of jurisdiction, 25 January 2000.

[22] Ibid., para. 56.

[23] Ibid., para. 62-63.

[24] *Siemens A.G. v. The Argentine Republic,* ICSID Case No. ARB/02/8, Decision on Jurisdiction, 3 August 2004.

[25] Ibid., para. 102.

[26] Ibid., para. 106.

[27] Paragraph 120.

[28] *Gas Natural SDG, S.A. and The Republic of Argentina,* ICSID Case No. ARB/03/10, Decision of the Tribunal on Preliminary Questions on Jurisdiction, 17 June 2005, para. 49.

[29] *Suez, Sociedad General de Aguas de Barcelona S.A., and InterAguas Servicios Integrales del Agua, S.A. v. The Republic of Argentina*, ICSID Case No. ARB/03/17, Decision on Jurisdiction of May 16, 2006, para. 57.

[30] *Camuzzi International S.A. v. The Republic of Argentina;* ICSID Case No. ARB/03/7, Decision of the Tribunal on Objections to Jurisdiction, 10 June 2005.

[31] *National Grid PLC v. Republic of Argentina,* UNCITRAL Arbitration, Decision on Jurisdiction, 20 June 2006.

[32] *AWG Group Ltd v. The Republic of Argentina,* UNCITRAL, Decision on Jurisdiction, 3 August 2006.

[33] That is, if something is not explicitly excluded by the MFN clause it should be deemed as covered.

[34] *Ibid.,* para. 62.

[35] *Ibid.,* para. 63.

[36] *Siemens v. Argentina,* op. cit, para. 107.

[37] *Gas Natural v. Argentina,* op. cit, para. 30

[38] *National Grid v. Argentina,* op. cit. para. 92.

[39] *Wintershall Aktiengesellschaft v. Argentine Republic,* ICSID Case No. ARB/04/14, Award, 8 December 2008.

[40] Ibid., para. 160(3).

[41] Ibid., para. 167

[42] Ibid., para. 185.

[43] Ibid., para. 186

[44] *Salini Costruttori S.p.A. and Italstrade S.p.A. and The Hasemite Kingdom of Jordan,* ICSID Case No. ARB/02/13, Decision on Jurisdiction, 29 November 2004.

[45] Ibid., para 115.

[46] Ibid., para. 118.

[47] *Plama Consortium Limited and Republic of Bulgaria,* ICSID Case No. ARB/03/04, Decision on Jurisdiction, 8 February 2005.

[48] Ibid., para. 208.

[49] Ibid., para. 209.

[50] Ibid., para. 212 and 219.

[51] Ibid., para. 223.

[52] *Telenor Mobile Communications A.S. and The Republic of Hungary,* ICSID Case No. ARB/04/15, Award, 13 September 2006.

[53] Ibid., para. 92 and 95.

[54] Ibid., para. 93-94.

[55] *Vladimir Berschader and Moise Berschader v. The Russian Federation,* Arbitration Institute of the Stockholm Chamber of Commerce, Case No. 080/2005, Award, 21 April 2006.

[56] Ibid., para. 178.

[57] Ibid., para. 181.

[58] *Tza Yap Shum v. The Republic of Peru,* ICSID Case No. ARB/07/6, Decision on Jurisdiction and Competence, 19 June 2009.

[59] Ibid., para. 196 and 198.

[60] Ibid., para. 216.

[61] See further: Gaillard (2005) and Kinnear (2005).

[62] *RosInvestCo UK Ltd. v. The Russian Federation,* Arbitration Institute of the Stockholm Chamber of Commerce, Case No. 079/2005, Award, October 2007.

[63] Ibid., para. 131.

[64] Ibid., para.131.

[65] Ibid., para. 132.

[66] *Renta 4S.V.S.A., et al v. The Russian Federation,* Arbitration Institute of the Stockholm Chamber of Commerce, Case. No. 024/2007, Award, 20 March 2009.

[67] Ibid., para. 92.

[68] Ibid., para. 119.

[69] See further: Faya-Rodriguez (2008) and Banifatemi (2008).

[70] Negotiations of the FTAA have not been concluded.

III. ASSESSMENT AND POLICY OPTIONS

Like other IIA provisions, MFN treatment clauses are negotiated in the context of the overall policy objective of IIAs, which is to achieve a balanced regime of investor/investment promotion and protection, in some cases also liberalization, through providing a stable, predictable and secure investment environment that also serves the development aims of host countries. Development objectives are pursued by way of attracting beneficial investment and by allowing sufficient policy space to permit effective and legitimate development policy to operate (UNCTAD 2003 and 2000b). On this main issue, the findings of the earlier edition of the IIA Issues Papers Series have not changed drastically over the last decade.

"The countries that apply liberal policies vis-à-vis foreign investors assume presumably that foreign investment is a means for increasing local productivity and competitiveness. The MFN standard has been an inherent part of their development policies, since after all an open-door policy means that no restrictions on, or discrimination between, foreign investors are in effect that are based on the nationality of the investor.

On the other hand, there have also been strategies of selective intervention. Countries pursuing these strategies seek to steer foreign investors into those activities they consider particularly important for their economic development. There is evidence that such a policy can contribute to an acceleration and deepening of the process of industrial development in particular. This approach requires the identification of activities in which a country can reasonably expect to acquire a comparative advantage and the promotion of production in such areas.

It may be argued that an exception to MFN based on the nationality of foreign investors would be consistent with the strategy of a host country that has made the judgment that the best way to pursue the economic development of the country is to establish and maintain special economic relations with one or several specific other countries, which would be selected as strategic partners. The countries concerned would thus grant market access or other special privileges only to investors from these countries. Such a strategy assumes that one or several countries with strategic advantages over other potential partners could be identified (and that granting the same conditions to investors from other countries would undermine this strategic partnership). The host country would align its own pattern of comparative advantages and its stage of development to the comparative advantages of the partner.

What is not clear is why obtaining the desired investment from one set of investors would be more desirable than obtaining them from another set of investors, as long as the underlying development objectives are being served. Rather, it would appear that strategies of this type are normally based on a distinction between foreign and domestic investors and not on a distinction among foreign investors." (UNCTAD 1999a)

This analysis holds true to date as far as investment strategies and policies are concerned and can continue to be taken into account by States when assessing the economic rationale of negotiating MFN treatment clauses of different kind in their treaties. No major changes have taken place in this regard.

In this context, however, the interpretations and applications of the MFN treatment clause by arbitral tribunals starting with the *Maffezini v. Spain* case have generated focus on MFN treatment clauses in IIAs lately and are at the origin of many strong reactions or doubts. These interpretations have raised concern and caution on the part of States having negotiated or in the process of negotiating IIAs. As indicated in the preceding sections, this particular aspect and scope of interpretation of MFN treatment was not at the heart of the priorities and concerns of negotiators before *Maffezini v. Spain.*

But much has changed since and all new implications must be taken into account.

As shown in the preceding analysis, recent treaties have approached the interpretation and application by arbitral tribunals of MFN treatment clauses in different manners. Some countries have shown concern with these interpretations and have reacted promptly, seeking to identify, clarify or reduce the scope of application of the MFN treatment clauses in their model treaties and negotiations. Other countries, having assessed the implications have come to the conclusion that these broad interpretations were in line with their expectations and did not bring notable changes to the formulation of the MFN treatment clauses in their model treaties and subsequent negotiations. However, the fact that a country has not reacted through changes in their model treaty or new treaty drafting does not necessarily mean an implicit agreement with the broad and furthermore inconsistent interpretations by arbitral tribunals

A majority of countries, particularly developing countries, are struggling with the scope and formulation of the MFN treatment clauses in IIAs and particularly with **three issues:** (a) inconsistent and conflicting interpretations of the scope of MFN treatment in ISDS cases; (b) inconsistent approaches and wording in their network of existing treaties, particularly with vague and broad wording in earlier treaties; and consequently (c) clear and certain ways to address these two challenges in their future negotiations and in their existing network of treaties.

Inconsistent and conflicting interpretations: The fundamental uncertainty about the scope of the MFN treatment obligation engendered by conflicting arbitral awards affects the States parties to IIAs when entering into MFN commitments, when dealing with an extensive network of treaties and of course when defending their interests in ISDS cases. But also importantly (and this is often overlooked), the uncertainty and ongoing discussions and debates affect investors who are left unclear about the way to use or invoke MFN treatment commitments made by their host State.

Inconsistent approaches and wording of MFN treatment provisions: This is particularly the case for developing countries that have been negotiating IIAs with various capital exporting countries, or have themselves turned from mainly capital importing to both capital importing and exporting countries. These countries generally have a network of treaties that have variations in the approaches to MFN treatment and sometimes considerable differences in the wording of the substantive protection or ISDS clauses. These variations are the result of the negotiation over time and with treaty partners having themselves different approaches or objectives. The uncertainty about the possible interpretation of MFN treatment and the possibly broad interpretation that would allow the importing of ISDS or other protection provisions from other IIAs is creating an additional challenge for developing countries as regards their network of existing treaties, the design or revision of their own models and ongoing negotiations of IIAs.

A majority of countries have in their network of IIAs treaties with vague, unclear or broad wording.[1] An important issue is therefore for countries to assess whether the language of these treaties is in line with their understanding and their approach to the commitment to grant MFN treatment or if not, how to deal with these provisions of earlier treaties.

A number of countries have embarked internally or called upon UNCTAD to assist them in a review of IIA commitments in the light of MFN treatment clauses in order to assess the extent of their commitments, highlight possible inconsistencies and risks and propose appropriate course of action.

It is important for States that have an extensive network of treaties and particularly for developing countries that have a network of treaties with a variety of approaches to identify the implications, assess the possible risks engendered by these approaches and then make informed decisions about their existing network of treaties and the future commitments. Given the importance of certainty and predictability for foreign investors but also for States entering into IIA commitments and in the context of broad or inconsistent interpretations by arbitral tribunals, this Section will now seek to assess the implications and propose some policy and negotiation options for policymakers and negotiators.

A. Implications for negotiators and policymakers when considering their MFN treatment policies

As noted in the first edition of this paper, the more foreign investors from various home countries invest in a host country, the more important the MFN treatment commitment becomes in order to ensure equality of opportunities for investors of different nationalities, either seeking to make an investment in the country or operating an investment established in accordance with the host country's laws and regulations (UNCTAD 1999a). Given that most economies are interlinked to the rest of the world and continuously seek to attract and retain foreign capital, MFN treatment continues to be an essential tool together with NT to ensure non-discriminatory treatment in the host country.

The role of MFN treatment in investment policies, and therefore also in IIAs, is less central than NT. In fact, States generally do not discriminate among foreign investors of different nationalities when it comes to the treatment they afford these investors once established. The main policy decisions relate to the protection of national investors or sectors of the national economy, therefore investment policies generally focus the distinction between national investors and foreign investors but not among foreigners of different nationalities.

With the notable exception of preferential regional arrangements (REIO), BITs or investment chapters of FTAs/regional trade agreements (RTAs) contain remarkably few reservations as far as pre-establishment MFN treatment is concerned because in fact there is no discrimination among foreign investors, with very few possible exceptions (e.g. specific sectors which entry is conditioned upon reciprocity). The role of MFN treatment here is to accompany NT not for purposes of liberalizing the entry regime but of ensuring that any future liberalization granted to a third treaty partner is extended to the investors of the beneficiary contracting State.

The granting of MFN treatment to a foreign investor/investment comes only with the conclusion of an IIA and requires special attention when assessing possible non-conforming measures or potential violations and recording them in the treaty. The scope of the MFN treatment clause as regards the beneficiary (investor and/or investment) and the investment-related activities it applies to (pre-post establishment, list of activities, broad approach), the enumeration of treaty articles, exceptions or specific qualifications relating to ISDS and other commitments are of particular importance.

MFN treatment clauses establish constraints upon host countries with regard to their present and future investment policies, particularly when pre-establishment rights are conferred. States may not change the rules of the game that easily. Even though the economic rationale behind a measure favouring a specific foreign investor over another foreign investor is weaker than that of favouring a national over a foreigner, there are cases in which States may wish to offer benefits to a restricted number of foreign beneficiaries, e.g. preferential deals with strategic partners, membership to economic arrangements, areas or sectors in which reciprocity is an important element or policies of selective intervention. In these cases, States can use specific or general exceptions.

With the proliferation of IIAs that include MFN treatment clauses, a vast majority of countries have a network of IIAs concluded over the last 20 years and that contain provisions (including MFN clauses) that can be of different type and wording. Some countries have standard REIO exceptions to the MFN treatment clause in the IIAs they concluded, while other countries do not have such exceptions. Some countries have consistently excluded taxation matters from the MFN treatment clause while others have limited this exception to obligations stemming from double-taxation agreements. Some countries have consistently used a list of investment related activities to define or clarify the substantive scope of MFN treatment; others have used wording extending MFN treatment to specific articles of the treaty itself or to "all matters" while other IIAs use wording by means of which MFN treatment is owed without further conditions or qualifications. Some countries have included a comparison requirement while others have not. Although the majority of countries have a separate and distinct MFN treatment obligation, others have linked it to the fair and equitable treatment commitment. The differences in the approaches must also be looked at with a time perspective, some countries having in their network a majority of "older" treaties while other countries have started the negotiation of IIAs more recently and would consequently have a more consistent approach to MFN treatment.

Given the interpretation by some arbitral tribunals to MFN treatment allowing to attract basically all treatment and protection provisions from third party treaties if the MFN treatment clause of the basic treaty does not specifically prevent it, an MFN treatment clause would possibly "multilateralize" all treaty commitments and make them available to any investor from a home country that has signed such provisions. While some see MFN treatment clauses as a positive factor that fosters uniformity in international investment relationships and favours multilateralism despite the apparent fragmentation of IIAs,[2] others see the countless possible combinations and rather unforeseeable consequences as seriously damaging the predictability, certainty and even legitimacy of the system and not achieving harmonization, particularly with the important number of early treaties.[3]

It is the very nature of an MFN treatment clause under public international law to extend commitments under treaties to other treaty partners. However, it is fair to say that the "broad" interpretation of MFN treatment clauses to allow the import of ISDS provisions from another treaty was not foreseen at the time the MFN clauses in question were negotiated. Although debated among practitioners and academics and sometimes challenged by arbitral tribunals in a significant number of cases, it is also fair to say that the *Maffezini v. Spain* interpretation came as a surprise to a number of negotiators and policymakers, as well as academics and practitioners of international investment law. The original purpose of such clauses was indeed to ensure competitive equality and avoid discriminatory treatment between foreign investors of different nationalities as regards their respective treatment afforded by the host State under its national laws, regulations and administrative decisions or by its actions, measures and practices.

Some arbitral awards have held that the content of an IIA itself can be considered at the root of competitive equality and can constitute the treatment afforded by the MFN treatment clause. In this case, a foreign investor protected by a treaty that has a broad ISDS provision can be considered in a better competitive position than an investor that is covered by a more restrictive treaty. It should be noted, however, that only few arbitral awards go to the extent of making this comparison.[4]

This interpretation is not convincing in many aspects, particularly as far as dispute settlement is concerned. It remains to be seen whether to date, settlement of a dispute by international arbitration is more favourable than the recourse to national courts or domestic arbitration. The perception of the early 1960s may not necessarily reflect reality. Investment protection treaties merely provide for compensation *ex post* for the violation by the State of a protection commitment and are not meant to seek the enforcement of a commitment other than by compensation. The settlement of an investment dispute, if decided in favour of the investor, results in the payment of monetary compensation and not in the withdrawal by the State of the measure or act that is affecting a foreign investor or any other redress or implementation. Moreover, the amount of compensation will take into account and bear interests from the day the alleged violation has occurred and therefore the date of the payment of this compensation would not make a major competitive difference to an investor that has been expropriated or that has not been treated in accordance with FET or a full protection and security standard. It may be of interest to an investor seeking a private insurance or a guarantee for political risk by a State or multilateral guarantee agency to benefit from a broad ISDS or other substantive protection provision, but the possibility to invoke another treaty provision is generally put forward only at the stage of an actual dispute and an ISDS case.

The borrowing or importing of substantive provisions from third treaties is also difficult and must be done carefully. Tribunals have held that the scope of application of the basic treaty is to remain intact. Likewise, reading out provisions contained in the basic treaty or attracting like provisions merely perceived as more favourable may not be feasible. But even when it comes to the borrowing of substantive provisions which are absent in the basic treaty (a notion accepted by the tribunals having dealt with this issue so far) some of the points referred to in the previous paragraph still apply. Assuming MFN treatment in investment agreements, the exercise should not entail an automatic importation but the undertaking of an assessment of whether the absence of the provision at stake actually causes a damage to the investor, for which the measure that gave rise to the dispute would have to be characterized as breaching said provision in the first place. Moreover, if the importing of a regime into the basic treaty notably disrupts the structure and nature of the latter, the outcome should be disregarded.

Should investors begin to seek *a priori* redress of MFN treatment violations clauses or enforcement by an arbitral tribunal, together with a partial rewriting of the basic BIT, then policymakers and negotiators would have to take this into account in future MFN treatment policies and treaty commitments.

B. Policy options

1. Defining the scope of application of the MFN treatment clause

Option 1: Application of MFN treatment to pre-establishment

States may wish to afford MFN treatment to the pre-establishment phase. This can be done by explicitly referring to establishment-related activities (e.g., "establishment, acquisition or expansion"). Under such circumstances, the entry regime is governed by the treaty itself and not by the domestic framework. When combined with NT pre-establishment commitments (as is usually the case), the system offers more transparency, certainty and predictability for the investment flows. Worth noting is that NT is much more central than MFN treatment for purposes of liberalizing the entry regime of the host State, given that most barriers of entry are measures inconsistent with NT and only a few with MFN treatment. In and of itself, the major role of MFN treatment here is to guarantee that any further liberalization as regards entry conditions offered to a third country will be extended to the investors of the beneficiary State. See Section II.A.1(ii) for examples and further details.

This approach, which is found in IIAs dealing with liberalization (e.g. FTAs/EPAs), effectively imposes upon host States important constraints as already explained. No discriminatory measures between investors that are based on their nationality are allowed. However, these effects may be mitigated through the inclusion of specific or generic exceptions, by means of which countries may retain a sound policy space and the flexibility to regulate specific activities or areas of their interest. See Section II.A.3.(ii) for examples and further details.

Option 2: Application of MFN treatment to post-establishment

Another policy option – the one most frequently used in BITs – is to apply the MFN clause to post-entry only. In this context the IIA would contain an "admission clause" and the MFN treatment clause will not refer to any establishment-related activities, resulting in a situation where the entry conditions are left to domestic regulatory prerogatives. This approach is appropriate when the IIA's objective is merely to protect FDI flows and not to liberalize. Additionally, from the negotiation perspective, this is a prudent approach when a State lacks the institutional capacity or finds it difficult to accurately identify all non-conforming measures or the exceptions it requires to keep for itself a sound policy space. The rational of MFN treatment here is weaker as opposed to the pre-establishment model, given that States normally do not discriminate amongst foreigners once they are established. However, it finds a role inasmuch the standard protects not only against "*de facto*" but also "*de iure*" discriminatory measures. See Section II.A.1.(i) for examples and further details).

Option 3: Application of the MFN clause to investors and/or investments

IIAs generally cover both investments and their investors, although there could be variants such as limiting the protection to investments. The latter approach diminishes the object and purpose of the IIA. But by the other token, it minimizes the exposure of the State to international liability, inter alia, because investments are qualified and defined by domestic law, may not possess legal personality (thus being subjected to a lesser universe of measures) and may not be able to claim via MFN treatment a number of privileges applicable only to investors (e.g. access to ISDS). However, this decision of subjective coverage seems less important as compared to the decision regarding the entry model and the inclusion of exceptions and qualifications. Moreover, practice is highly uniform as to include both investors and investments within MFN treatment and no significant problems have arisen as a consequence thereof. See Section II.A.2 for examples and further details.

Option 4: Systemic exceptions

Many MFN clauses in BITs contain reciprocal, subject-specific exceptions. The most common of these systemic exceptions, particularly when it comes to post-establishment IIAs, are the REIO and taxation exceptions (see Section II.A.3.(i) for examples and further details). Essentially they aim at preventing benefits under such treaties from passing to investors/investments of non-parties. In both cases, the application of MFN treatment would nullify the very idea underlying the agreement for which an exception is sought (regional economic integration or elimination of double taxation). Exceptions for regional integration processes might be particularly important for preserving and strengthening South-South integration. Hence, where parties want to retain control of existing arrangements, they may specify that the benefits conferred by certain current arrangements are not covered by the MFN treatment clause. This could be particularly helpful for maintaining intra-regional arrangements, especially between developing countries.

Option 5: Country/sector-specific exceptions

Other IIAs (notably those granting pre-establishment rights) include exceptions of different type, based on (a) specific development policy/regulatory concerns on areas such as intellectual property rights, subsidies, grants and governmental procurement; (b) the need to preserve certain existing non-conforming measures stemming from the domestic legal regime at the time the treaty is being negotiated; and (c) the need to preserve the full ability to regulate certain areas or sectors in the future. Other exceptions may include, for instance, concerns on culture, minority groups and land. As noted already, these exceptions somehow offset the limits that the pre-establishment model imposes upon States. See Section II.A.3.(ii) for examples and further details.

2. Dealing with other treaties

As explained in this paper, a broad approach towards the application of MFN treatment poses numerous policy challenges. It also may deviate from the original objective of such obligation. By automatically incorporating commitments from third treaties, a broad MFN obligation might practically ignore the sovereign freedom of States so conclude international obligations as they see fit. This may partially modify or nullify the basic treaty by means of importation of provisions from a third party treaty and may also create a sense of uniformity of standards when real variations in scope, content and intent exist for very good policy reasons. Even more so, it might be in conflict with the actual policy balance present in the IIA in question.

A broad MFN obligation can also make it hard to predict the extent of host country liabilities, as the applicable protection and ISDS provisions will be contingent on the perception of each investor, case by case, as well on a number of combinations and permutations actually impossible to foresee or administer. The approach also makes it difficult to update, refine or improve new IIAs, as the new treaties may be modified by reason of past treaties.

The core matter is that States should be able to have what they wish when entering into their commitments. Within this possibility of broad and unrestricted interpretations, different options arise. In particular, States may wish to specifically address the interaction of the MFN treatment clause with their net of IIAs.

Option 1: Extending MFN treatment to all treaties

This approach results in an MFN treatment obligation that covers both the treatment a host State accords domestically as well as the treatment offered in IIAs. This option is suitable for States seeking to maximize the protection or liberalization offered by their IIAs. It extends by reference the higher standards of treatment and procedural protection in other IIAs to which they are parties. This option requires that States do not have any objections to "treaty shopping" and any of the effects this might bring about.

These comprehensive and far-reaching effects result from an MFN clause which explicitly indicates that the MFN treatment clause extends commitments contained in third treaties. It is rare to see examples of MFN treatment clauses in IIAs explicitly extending to all treaties, although examples can be found in the context of regional arrangements (see box 17). These effects may also result, sometimes unintentionally, from an MFN treatment clause with a somewhat vague formulation (e.g. very short and unqualified formulation, reference to "all matters" or to the articles of the IIA in question. See for instance box 22). In the latter case, it is the lack of clarity and precision that facilitates expansionist interpretations. Thereby, such language raises fundamental issues about transparency, predictability and stability of the investment regime, as it may produce unintended and unforeseeable outcomes.

Option 2: Excluding other treaties from MFN treatment for pre-establishment and/or post-establishment purposes

Particularly in the context of liberalization treaties (i.e. pre-establishment), the broad approach also raises issues depending on whether MFN treatment applies to past and/or future treaties. MFN treatment may practically nullify the carefully crafted liberalization, pre-establishment or market access commitments at a bilateral level, effectively altering the balance of rights and obligations that underlies a particular treaty. It may also be difficult for the State to know with certainty the commitments it made in the past together with their possible interpretation. Thus, States may wish to exclude all prior treaties as to preserve the integrity of the negotiated entry regime. Moreover, States may also wish to exclude future treaties as well, with the aim of not extending without reaping something in return the benefits granted to other treaty partners, although in doing so the State may also lose the benefits granted to third treaty partners by its counterpart. The fact is that MFN treatment plays an important role as regards further liberalization undertaken by any of the contracting States (hence excluding future treaties from MFN treatment may be difficult). Alternatively, countries may provide that the benefits conferred by future liberalization or special arrangements would be subject to further negotiation with the aim of incorporating such benefits into the basic treaty (see for instance box 18). In any case, it is advisable to exclude all previous treaties as well as future treaties dealing with certain sectors regulated under reciprocity grounds such as aviation, fisheries and maritime matters including salvage (see for instance box 16).

For post-establishment purposes, the role of MFN treatment is less important, as already noted. As the different arbitral decisions show, only two cases have dealt with an actual comparing in treatment and the rest have involved treaty shopping. Therefore, States could consider excluding all treaties, past and future, for post-establishment purposes. This would allow focusing MFN treatment in a comparison in treatment together with a full respect of the various protection and ISDS provisions of the basic treaty. MFN still would play its function of guaranteeing a level field amongst foreign investors in like circumstances. This of course allows States to negotiate different content in the context of different negotiations and circumstances. Formulas such as the following may be used to this effect:

Option 1 (limiting the scope of application of MFN treatment in post-establishment)

1. [MFN treatment clause].

2. The obligation referred to in paragraph 1 above shall not apply to treatment accorded under all treaties, whether bilateral or multilateral, in force or signed prior to or after the date of entry into force of this Agreement.

Option 2 (clarifying the scope of application of MFN treatment in post-establishment)

1. [MFN treatment clause].
2. For greater certainty, the obligation referred to in paragraph 1 above shall not apply to treatment accorded under all treaties, whether bilateral or multilateral, in force or signed prior to or after the date of entry into force of this Agreement.

Given the two-fold nature of MFN treatment (whether in the context of liberalization or protection) a combination may be used in those IIAs with both pre-establishment and post-establishment (notably EPAs/FTAs). For pre-establishment purposes: excluding past treaties and certain future treaties; for post-establishment purposes: excluding all treaties, past and future. This combined approach would be accomplished though a special Annex such as the one shown below:

Annex to the MFN treatment clause

1. Article [MFN treatment clause] shall not apply to treatment accorded under all treaties, whether bilateral or multilateral, in force or signed prior to the date of entry into force of this Agreement.

3. Article [MFN treatment clause] shall not apply, as regards [post-establishment activities], to treatment accorded under all treaties, whether bilateral or multilateral, in force or signed after the date of entry into force of this Agreement.

3. Article [MFN treatment clause] shall not apply, as regards [pre-establishment activities], to treatment accorded under all treaties, whether bilateral or multilateral, in force or signed after the date of entry into force of this Agreement, dealing with the following issues: [listing relevant areas, e.g. the establishing, strengthening or expanding a free trade area or customs union; relating to aviation; fisheries; maritime matters, including salvage].

---

3. Clarifying the scope of application of MFN treatment with restrictive effects

When faced with the negotiation of a new agreement, States that are not comfortable with a wide approach to MFN treatment may wish to devise a number of restrictive formulations that clarify the operation of the MFN treatment clause. In this way, the contracting parties can confirm explicitly their actual intent.

Particular qualifications can be introduced as part of wording of the MFN clause itself or by way of an explanatory footnote or in an appendix/annex that forms part of the treaty. Such qualifications can be drafted "for greater certainty" purposes, i.e. the qualification is supposed to be implicit but it is made explicit. This approach is also helpful when States do not want to disrupt the manner in which other treaties may be interpreted. Carefully addressing the MFN issue in any revision of the country's model BIT can also play a role in this context.

States may use clarifications in order to assure that MFN treatment is interpreted and applied as they actually intend. This approach aims at avoiding ambiguity by explicitly addressing, i.e. clarifying, the scope of the MFN obligation. Clear language can serve to restrain unwarranted arbitral discretion. It can help ensure that the MFN clause is interpreted according to negotiating parties' agreed policy choices as expressed in the agreement. Several approaches can be taken.

Option 1: Specifying the activities to which treatment applies

One variation in this approach is to link the "treatment" owed to investors/investments to *a specific set of activities*. Treaty language could specifically list the activities concerned (e.g., establishment, acquisition, expansion, etc.) and/or include an explanation of what is meant by treatment under IIAs (see Section II.A.4.(ii) for examples and further details). This approach emphasizes that MFN treatment applies to the life-cycle of the investment. It should be noted however (as illustrated by arbitral practice) that this approach would not ensure specific outcomes, such as the applicability or not of MFN treatment to ISDS provisions.

Option 2: Specifying the nature of "treatment"

Another variation is to use more focused wording for what is treatment as it relates to *measures taken by the State*. This could be done by specifically referring to laws, regulations, administrative practices etc. or by pointing out that treatment is to be understood in the context of a country's laws and regulations applying to investors. This approach would strengthen the idea that MFN treatment requires an actual comparison between the treatment two foreign investors receive on a given scenario and not an ex ante treaty shopping operation. This approach may be accomplished by means of the following formula:

---

1. [MFN treatment clause].

2. For greater certainty, the obligation referred to in paragraph 1 above shall apply with respect to treatment accorded by a Contracting Party through the application of measures.

Further, a definition of "measures" may be included. In this context, Article 1 of the Canada-Peru BIT (2006) define measures as including any law, regulation, procedure, requirement, or practice.

Option 3: Specifying what would constitute unequal or "less favourable" treatment

Parties to investment treaties are also at liberty to define upfront what would be measures considered non-conforming to the obligation to extend MFN treatment to the investor. This is what several States have done in their annexes of non-conforming measures, listing those existing measures that are not in line with the MFN obligation. As indicated above, very few measures are specifically listed in these annexes. Their description however can provide a guidance to arbitral tribunals as to what elements and criteria should be looked at to assess non-conformity or violation of these provisions. Clearer language in the MFN treatment clause itself can also be used, such as in the Egypt-Germany BIT (2005) in its article 3.2:

"[…] *The following shall, in particular, be deemed 'treatment less favourable' within the meaning of this Article: unequal treatment in the case of restrictions on the purchase of raw or auxiliary materials, of energy or fuel or of means of production or operation of any kind, unequal treatment in the case of impeding the marketing of products inside or outside the country, as well as any other measures having similar effects. Measures that have to be taken for reasons of public security and order, public health or morality shall not be deemed 'treatment less favourable' within the meaning of this Article.*"

Option 4: Qualifiers such as "like circumstances"

A further consideration in the use of general, broad MFN clauses is whether to include an express reference to the issue of comparison though the "like circumstances" or the "like investors" formula (see Section II.A.4.(i) for examples and further details). As noted above, this is implicit in the MFN standard. But an explicit reference would remind arbitral tribunals that there has to be a comparative context when assessing an alleged breach. Comparing what it is reasonably comparable is fundamental so as to serve the object and purpose of guaranteeing competitive equality.

Option 5: Clarifying that MFN treatment does not apply to procedural and/or substantive provisions

Where parties want to avoid treaty shopping, whether for ISDS or substantive provisions, language may be included to that effect. Hence a tribunal would be prevented from importing third content or substituting basic content. This qualification may be partial, by specifying to which specific provisions of the treaty the MFN treatment clause applies or does not apply. This approach has been taken more recently by many countries as regards ISDS provisions. Indeed, in the aftermath of *Maffezini v. Spain,* many countries started including in their IIAs clarification notes as to exclude ISDS from MFN treatment (see Section II.D. for examples and further details).

The exclusion of certain or all provisions of the treaty may be accomplished through the use of formulas such as the following, where Option 1 refers to specific provisions whereas Option 2 ensures that the basic content remains intact.

Option 1

1. [MFN treatment clause].

2. For greater certainty, the obligation referred to in paragraph 1 above shall not apply to [articles/section] of this Agreement.

Option 2

1. [MFN treatment clause].

2. For greater certainty, the obligation referred to in paragraph 1 above shall apply without prejudice to the provisions set forth in this Agreement.

---

4. No MFN treatment clause

Another option would be to not include any MFN clause into the IIA. In international trade relations, an MFN clause may confer precise and specific economic advantages. With respect to IIAs, however, the positive, investment-enhancing inclusion of an MFN clause is less important as opposed to other provisions. This derives from the fact that States rarely discriminate amongst foreigners, out of specific preferential or economic arrangements with strategic partners. In fact, MFN treatment is only one of a large set of factors determining a company's investment decision, and hence it would be a fair decision for a State to decide that the inclusion of an MFN clause brings about more risks than benefits. Refraining from the inclusion of an MFN clause into an IIA also takes account of the differences between a clearly multilateral regime and a regime that is atomized and multi-layered, as is the case with the spaghetti bowl of IIAs. In the multilateral system of international trade rules, MFN is clearly a cornerstone of the system. In the particular context of BITs, where the treaties are designed and negotiated to suit the bilateral relationship between the respective contracting parties, the role of the MFN clause can, instead, be questioned.

However, it must be noted that, although not essential, MFN treatment still plays an important role for both liberalization and protection purposes. Also, the risks of treaty shopping may be effectively mitigated through limits to the scope of application, exclusion of third treaties or specific qualifications, as the preceding subsections have already noted.

5. Addressing the past vis-à-vis preserving the future

MFN clauses permitting treaty shopping can raise numerous fundamental policy and legal issues. Accordingly, States may wish to ensure that any MFN clauses in future BITs do not pave the way for what are considered unanticipated and/or undesirable effects. The problematic is, however, exacerbated by the fact that 2,750 BITs already exist, usually containing an MFN clause. Policymakers wishing to adopt a more focused and nuanced approach to MFN in the future may therefore also need to consider options for dealing with those MFN treatment clauses contained in IIAs already in force.

Current MFN treatment clauses will continue to constitute the majority of clauses potentially to be interpreted in ISDS cases. However, the fact that they have been negotiated already does not preclude the States from taking certain actions towards clarifying their scope and functioning. Amongst others, the following options arise.

The first is a bilateral exercise. States may amend treaties, although this can be difficult and time-consuming. The use of joint interpretations may be preferable, though the impact of an interpretative note may not be so great if this possibility was not foreseen in the treaty. Some treaties, however, set forth that any interpretation by the contracting parties of a provision of the treaty shall be binding on any tribunal. This possibility has been very useful in the context of the NAFTA (1992). But the parties to a treaty do not really need a provision of that sort in order to issue an interpretation with legal effects. The general rule of interpretation of the Vienna Convention on the Law of Treaties takes into account "any subsequent agreement between the parties regarding the interpretation of the treaty or the application of its provisions" (Article 31.3a). Likewise, "a special meaning shall be given to a term if it is established that the parties so intended" (Article 31.4).

The second approach is unilateral. Unilateral statements have an interpretative value, especially when they have been rendered outside a litigation context. Such statements reflect the intent of a Contracting Party. They have limits, however – they cannot change the text of the treaty and have to be part of a broader interpretative exercise. But they are very useful for discovering the content of a specific provision. For instance, some treaties, when sent to the approval of the internal legislative body, come with implementation statements or supportive documentation of an often informative character.

Other options include, amongst others, participation in the *deliberations of international organizations*, formal positions and specific objections upon certain issues. States that are uncomfortable with the way certain issues are being resolved can raise their voices. Such voices may have a legal effect which would constitute part of the context that arbitrators may need to consider when ascertaining the true intent behind the treaty. However, a danger in such a process is that States may *adopt opportunistic statements of interpretation* as a hedge against future or pending litigation. In such cases, the interpretative statement would be of little probative value. The work of the International Law Commission can also play a role in this context.

* * *

In sum, when assessing their treaty commitments and negotiating new treaties, States should consider the MFN treatment clause mindful of the overall balance between investment promotion, protection and/or liberalization objectives and a necessary space to develop policies and measures in line with their national priorities. This may be achieved through cautious and well-informed negotiations based on clear, balanced and well-defined definitions, concepts, rules and standards, as well as the proper use of exceptions, reservations, qualifications and/or carve-outs as to meet the particular needs of each contracting party.

States should also consider dealing with MFN treatment clauses in older treaties that are either not clear in their scope or do simply not reflect the intention of the parties when negotiating the treaty, mostly because the effect of such wording was not considered problematic at that time. In order to do so, States could give joint or unilateral interpretation of the formulation or clarify and delimit the scope of the MFN provision by means of a protocol or a revised formulation.

Notes

[1] The Argentina-Spain BIT (1991) for example states that "[...] 2. **In all matters subject to this Agreement**, this treatment shall be no less favourable than that extended by each Party to the investments made in its territory by investors of a third country. [...]" (non-official translation from Spanish, emphasis added).

[2] See for instance Schill, 2009.

[3] See *Plama v. Bulgaria* and *Telenor v. Hungary*.

[4] See further Fietta (2005), Freyer and Herlihy (2005).

REFERENCES

Aust, A. (2000). *Modern Treaty Law and Practice* (Cambridge: University Press).

Banifatemi, Y. (2008). "The emerging jurisprudence on the most-favoured-nation treatment in investment arbitration", in Andrea K Bjorklund, Ian A Laird and Sergey Ripinsky (eds.), *Investment Treaty Law, Current Issues III* (London: British Institute of International and Comparative Law), pp. 239-272.

Brownlie, I. (2003). *Principles of Public International Law* (Oxford: University Press).

Dixon, M. and McCorquodale, R. (2003). *Cases and Materials on International Law* (Oxford: University Press).

Dolzer, R. and Schreuer, C. (2008). *Principles of International Investment Law* (Oxford: University Press).

Faya-Rodriguez, A. (2008). "The most-favored-nation clause in international investment agreements: A tool for treaty shopping?", *Journal of International Arbitration*, Vol. 25, No. 1, pp. 89–102.

Fietta, S. (2005). "Most favoured nation treatment and dispute resolution under bilateral investment treaties: a turning point?", *International Arbitration Law Review*, Issue No. 4, pp. 131-138.

Freyer, D. H. and Herlihy, D. (2005). "Most-favored-nation treatment and dispute settlement in investment arbitration: Just how "favored" is "most-favored"?", *ICSID Review-Foreign Investment Law Journal*, Vol. 20, No. 1, pp. 58-83.

Gaillard, E. (2005). "Establishing jurisdiction through a most-favored-nation clause", *New York Law Journal: International Arbitration Law*, Vol. 233, No. 105 (June), pp. 1-3.

International Law Commission (ILC) (1978). "Draft articles on most-favoured-nation", in *Yearbook of the International Law Commission*, Vol. II, Part Two. Available at: http://untreaty.un.org/ilc/texts/instruments/english/draft%20articles/ 1_3_1978.pdf.

Joubin-Bret, A. (2008). "Admission and establishment in the context of investment protection", in August Reinisch (ed.), *Standards of Investment Protection* (Oxford: University Press), pp. 9-28.

Kinnear, M., Bjorklund, A. K. and Hannaford, J. F..G. (2006). "Article 1103: most-favored-nation treatment", in M. Kinnear, A.K. Bjorklund and J.F.G. Hannaford (eds.). *Investment Disputes Under NAFTA: An Annotated Guide to NAFTA* (La Haya: Kluwer), (Chapter XI).

Koskenniemi, M. (1989). *From Apology to Utopia: The Structure of International Legal Argument* (Helsinki: University of Helsinki).

Kurtz, J. (2005). "The delicate extension of MFN treatment to foreign investors: Maffezini v. Kingdom of Spain", in T. Weiler (ed.), *International Investment Law and Arbitration: Leading Cases from the ICSID, NAFTA, Bilateral Treaties and Customary International Law* (London: Cameron May), pp. 523-556.

McLachlan, C., Shore, L., and Weiniger, M. (2007). *International Investment Arbitration: Substantive Principles* (Oxford: University Press).

Muchlinski, P. T. (2007). *Multinational Enterprises and the Law* (Oxford: University Press).

Organisation for Economic Cooperation and Development (OECD) (1998). *Commentary to the Consolidated Text of the Multilateral*

Agreement on Investment, Document No. DAFFE/MAI(98)8/REV1 (Paris: OECD).

Rubins, N. (2008). "MFN Clauses, Procedural Rights and a Return to the Treaty Text", in T. Weiler, *Investment Treaty Arbitration and International Law* (New York: Juris Publishing), Chapter 10.

Schill, S. W. (2009). "Multilateralizing investment treaties through most-favoured-nation clauses", *Berkeley Journal of International Law*, Vol. 27, No. 2. pp. 496-569.

Teitelbaum, R. (2005). "Who's afraid of Maffezini? Recent developments in the interpretation of most favored nation clauses", *Journal of International Arbitration*, Vol. 22, No. 3, pp 225-237.

United Nations Conference on Trade and Development (UNCTAD) (1999a). *Most-Favoured-Nation Treatment. UNCTAD Series on Issues in International Investment Agreements* (New York and Geneva: United Nations), United Nations publication, Sales No. E.99.II.D.11.Available at:
http://www.unctad.org/en/docs/psiteiitd10v3.en.pdf.

_____ (1999b). *Scope and Definition. Series on Issues in International Investment Agreements* (New York and Geneva: United Nations), United Nations publication, Sales No. E.99.II.D.9. Available at: http://www.unctad.org/en/docs/psiteiitd11v2.en.pdf.

_____ (2000a). *Taxation. Series on Issues in International Investment Agreements* (New York and Geneva: United Nations), United Nations publication, Sales No. E.00.II.D.5. Available at: http://www.unctad.org/en/docs/iteiit16_en.pdf.

_____ (2000b). *Flexibility for Development. Series on Issues in International Investment Agreements* (New York and Geneva: United Nations), United Nations publication, Sales No. E.00.II.D.6. Available at: http://www.unctad.org/en/docs/psiteiitd18.en.pdf.

_____ (2003). *World Investment Report 2003. FDI Policies for Development: National and International Perspectives* (New York and Geneva: United Nations), United Nations Publication, Sales No. E.03.II.D.8. Available at: http://www.unctad.org/en/docs/wir2003_en.pdf.

_____ (2004a). *The REIO Exception in MFN Treatment Clauses. Series on International Investment Policies for Development* (New York and Geneva: United Nations), United Nations publication, Sales No. 05.II.D.1. Available at: http://www.unctad.org/en/docs/iteiit20047_en.pdf.

_____ (2004b). *International Investment Agreements: Key Issues.* Volume I (New York and Geneva: United Nations), United Nations publication, Sales No. E.05.II.D.6. Available at: http://www.unctad.org/en/docs/iteiit200410_en.pdf.

_____ (2006). *Preserving Flexibility in IIAs: The Use of Reservations. Series on International Investment Policies for Development* (New York and Geneva: United Nations), United Nations publication, Sales No. E.06.II.D.14. Available at: http://www.unctad.org/en/docs/iteiit20058_en.pdf.

_____ (2009). "Recent developments in international investment agreements (2008–June 2009)", *IIA Monitor*, No. 3. Available at: http://www.unctad.org/en/docs/webdiaeia20098_en.pdf.

_____ (2010). *World Investment Report 2010. Investing in a Low-carbon Economy* (New York and Geneva: United Nations), United Nations Publication, Sales No. E.10.II.D.2. Available at: http://www.unctad.org/en/docs/wir2010_en.pdf

_____ (forthcoming). *Scope and Definition: A Sequel. UNCTAD Series on International Investment Agreements II* (New York and Geneva: United Nations), United Nations publication, forthcoming.

WTO (2004). *Consultative Board. The Future of the WTO: Addressing Institutional Challenges in the New Millennium* (Geneva: WTO).

CASES AND ARBITRAL AWARDS

ADF Group Inc. v. The United States of America, ICSID Case No. ARB(AF)/00/1, Award, 9 January 2003.

Ambiatelos Claim (Greece v. United Kingdom), 2 March 1956 (1956 *International Law Reports* 306).

Archer Daniels Midland Company v. the United Mexican States, ICSID Case No. ARB(AF)/04/05, Award, 21 November 2007.

Asian Agricultural Products Ltd. (AAPL) v. Republic of Sri Lanka, ICSID Case No. ARB/87/3, Final Award, 27 June 1990.

AWG Group Ltd v. The Republic of Argentina, UNCITRAL, Decision on Jurisdiction, 3 August 2006.

Bayindir Insaat Turizm Ticaret Ve Sanayi AS v. Islamic Republic of Pakistan, ICSID Case No. ARB/03/29, Award, 27 August 2009.

Bayindir Insaat Turizm Ticaret Ve Sanayi AS v. Islamic Republic of Pakistan, ICSID Case No. ARB/03/29, Decision on Jurisdiction, 14 November 2005.

Camuzzi International S.A. v. The Republic of Argentina; ICSID Case No. ARB/03/7, Decision of the Tribunal on Objections to Jurisdiction, 10 June 2005.

Champion Trading Company Ameritrade International, Inc. v. Republic of Egypt, ICSID Case No. ARB/02/09, Award, 27 October 2006.

CME Czech Republic B.V. v. The Czech Republic, UNCITRAL, Final Award, 14 March 2003.
CMS Gas Transmission Company v. The Argentine Republic, ICSID Case No. ARB/01/08, Award, 25 April 2005.

Corn Products International Inc. v. the United Mexican States, ICSID Case No. ARB(AF)/04/01, Decision on Responsibility, 15 January 2008.

Emilio Agustín Maffezini and The Kingdom of Spain, ICSID Case No. ARB/97/7, Decision of the tribunal on the objections of jurisdiction, 25 January 2000.

Gas Natural SDG, S.A. and The Republic of Argentina, ICSID Case No. ARB/03/10, Decision of the Tribunal on Preliminary Questions on Jurisdiction, 17 June 2005.

Marvin Feldman v. Mexico, ICSID Case No. ARB(AF)/99/1, Award, 16 December 2002.

M.C.I. Power Group L.C. and New Urbine, Inc. V. Republic of Ecuador, ICSID Case No. ARB/03/6, Award, 31 July 2007.

Methanex Corporation v. United States of America, UNCITRAL, Final Award on Jurisdiction and Merits, 3 August 2005.

Mihaly International Corporation v. Sri Lanka, ICSID Case No. ARB/00/2, Award, 15 March 2002.

MTD Equity Sdn. Bhd. & MTD Chile S.A. v. Chile, ICSID Case No. ARB/01/7, Award, 25 May 2004.

Nagel v. Czech Republic, SCC Case 49/2002, Award, 2003.

National Grid PLC v. Republic of Argentina, UNCITRAL Arbitration, Decision on Jurisdiction, 20 June 2006.

Parkerings-Compagniet AS v. Republic of Lithuania, ICSID Case No. ARB/05/8, Award, 11 September 2007.

Plama Consortium Limited and Republic of Bulgaria, ICSID Case No. ARB/03/04, Decision on Jurisdiction, 8 February 2005.

Pope & Talbot Inc. v. Canada, Award on the Merits of Phase 2, 10 April 2001.

Renta 4S.V.S.A., et al v. The Russian Federation, Arbitration Institute of the Stockholm Chamber of Commerce, Case. No. 024/2007, Award, 20 March 2009.

RosInvestCo UK Ltd. v. The Russian Federation, Arbitration Institute of the Stockholm Chamber of Commerce, Case No. 079/2005, Award, October 2007.

Salini Costruttori S.p.A. and Italstrade S.p.A. and The Hasemite Kingdom of Jordan, ICSID Case No. ARB/02/13, Decision on Jurisdiction, 29 November 2004.

S.D. Myers Inc. v. Canada, UNCITRAL, Award, 2002.

Siemens A.G. v. The Argentine Republic, ICSID Case No. ARB/02/8, Decision on Jurisdiction, 3 August 2004.

Société Generale v. The Dominican Republic, LCAI Case No. UN 7927, Award on Preliminary Objections to Jurisdiction.

Suez, Sociedad General de Aguas de Barcelona S.A., and InterAguas Servicios Integrales del Agua, S.A. v. The Republic of Argentina, ICSID Case No. ARB/03/17, Decision on Jurisdiction, 16 May 2006.

Tecnicas Mediambientales Tecmed S.A. v. the United Mexican States, ICSID Case no. ARB (AF)/00/02, Award, 29 May 2003.

Telenor Mobile Communications A.S. v. The Republic of Hungary, ICSID Case No. ARB/04/15, Award, 13 September 2006.

TSA Spectrum de Argentina S.A. v. Argentine Republic, ICSID Case No. ARB/05/05, Award, 19 December 2009.

Tza Yap Shum v. The Republic of Peru, ICSID Case No. ARB/07/6, Decision on Jurisdiction and Competence, 19 June 2009.

United Parcel Service of America Inc. v. Government of Canada, Award on the Merits, 24 May 2007.

Vladimir Berschader and Moise Berschader v. The Russian Federation, Arbitration Institute of the Stockholm Chamber of Commerce, Case No. 080/2005, Award, 21 April 2006.

Wintershall Aktiengesellschaft v. Argentine Republic, ICSID Case No. ARB/04/14, Award, 8 December 2008.

SELECTED UNCTAD PUBLICATIONS ON INTERNATIONAL INVESTMENT AGREEMENTS, TRANSNATIONAL CORPORATIONS AND FOREIGN DIRECT INVESTMENT

(For more information, please visit www.unctad.org/en/pub)

World Investment Reports
(For more information visit www.unctad.org/wir)

World Investment Report 2010. Investing in a Low-Carbon Economy. Sales No. E.10.II.D.1. $80. http://www.unctad.org/en/docs//wir2010_en.pdf.

World Investment Report 2009. Transnational Corporations, Agricultural Production and Development. Sales No. E.09.II.D.15. $80. http://www.unctad.org/en/docs/wir2009_en.pdf.

World Investment Report 2008. Transnational Corporations and the Infrastructure Challenge. Sales No. E.08.II.D.23. $80. http://www.unctad.org/en/docs//wir2008_en.pdf.

World Investment Report 2007. Transnational Corporations, Extractive Industries and Development. Sales No. E.07.II.D.9. $75. http://www.unctad.org/ en/docs//wir2007_en.pdf.

World Investment Report 2006. FDI from Developing and Transition Economies: Implications for Development. Sales No. E.06.II.D.11. $75. http://www.unctad.org/ en/docs//wir2006_en.pdf.

World Investment Report 2005. Transnational Corporations and the Internationalization of R&D. Sales No. E.05.II.D.10. $75. http://www.unctad.org/ en/docs//wir2005_en.pdf.

World Investment Report 2004. The Shift Towards Services. Sales No. E.04.II.D.36. $75. http://www.unctad.org/en/docs//wir2004_en.pdf.

World Investment Report 2003. FDI Policies for Development: National and International Perspectives. Sales No. E.03.II.D.8. $49. http://www.unctad.org/en/docs//wir2003_en.pdf.

World Investment Report 2002: Transnational Corporations and Export Competitiveness. 352 p. Sales No. E.02.II.D.4. $49. http://www.unctad.org/en/docs//wir2002_en.pdf.

World Investment Report 2001: Promoting Linkages. 356 p. Sales No. E.01.II.D.12 $49. http://www.unctad.org/wir/contents/wir01content.en.htm.

World Investment Report 2000: Cross-border Mergers and Acquisitions and Development. 368 p. Sales No. E.99.II.D.20. $49. http://www.unctad.org/wir/contents/wir00content.en.htm.

Ten Years of World Investment Reports: The Challenges Ahead. Proceedings of an UNCTAD special event on future challenges in the area of FDI. UNCTAD/ITE/Misc.45. http://www.unctad.org/wir.

International Investment Policies for Development
(For more information visit http://www.unctad.org/iia)

The Role of International Investment Agreements in Attracting Foreign Direct Investment to Developing Countries. 161 p. Sales no. E.09.II.D.20. $22.

The Protection of National Security in IIAs. 170 p. Sales no. E.09.II.D.12. $15.

Identifying Core Elements in Investment Agreements in the APEC Regions. 134 p. Sales no. E.08.II.D.27. $15.

International Investment Rule-Making: Stocktaking, Challenges and the Way Forward. 124 p. Sales no. E.08.II.D.1. $15.

Investment Promotion Provisions in International Investment Agreements. 103 p. Sales no. E.08.II.D.5. $15.

Investor-State Dispute Settlement and Impact on Investment Rulemaking. 110 p. Sales No. E.07.II.D.10. $30.

Bilateral Investment Treaties 1995—2006: Trends in Investment Rulemaking. 172 p. Sales No. E.06.II.D.16. $30.

Investment Provisions in Economic Integration Agreements. 174 p. UNCTAD/ITE/IIT/2005/10.

Preserving Flexibility in IIAs: The Use of Reservations. 104 p. Sales no.: E.06.II.D.14. $15.

International Investment Arrangements: Trends and Emerging Issues. 110 p. Sales No. E.06.II.D.03. $15.

Investor-State Disputes Arising from Investment Treaties: A Review. 106 p. Sales No. E.06.II.D.1 $15

South-South Cooperation in Investment Arrangements. 108 p. Sales No. E.05.II.D.26 $15.

International Investment Agreements in Services. 119 p. Sales No. E.05.II.D.15. $15.

The REIO Exception in MFN Treatment Clauses. 92 p. Sales No. E.05.II.D.1. $15.

Issues in International Investment Agreements
(For more information visit http://www.unctad.org/iia)

International Investment Agreements: Key Issues, Volumes I, II and *III.* Sales no.: E.05.II.D.6. $65.

State Contracts. 84 p. Sales No. E.05.II.D.5. $15.

Competition. 112 p. E.04.II.D.44. $ 15.

Key Terms and Concepts in IIAs: a Glossary. 232 p. Sales No. E.04.II.D.31. $15.

Incentives. 108 p. Sales No. E.04.II.D.6. $15.

Transparency. 118 p. Sales No. E.04.II.D.7. $15.

Dispute Settlement: State-State. 101 p. Sales No. E.03.II.D.6. $15.

Dispute Settlement: Investor-State. 125 p. Sales No. E.03.II.D.5. $15.

Transfer of Technology. 138 p. Sales No. E.01.II.D.33. $18.

Illicit Payments. 108 p. Sales No. E.01.II.D.20. $13.

Home Country Measures. 96 p. Sales No.E.01.II.D.19. $12.

Host Country Operational Measures. 109 p. Sales No E.01.II.D.18. $15.

Social Responsibility. 91 p. Sales No. E.01.II.D.4. $15.

Environment. 105 p. Sales No. E.01.II.D.3. $15.

Transfer of Funds. 68 p. Sales No. E.00.II.D.27. $12.

Flexibility for Development. 185 p. Sales No. E.00.II.D.6. $15.

Employment. 69 p. Sales No. E.00.II.D.15. $12.

Taxation. 111 p. Sales No. E.00.II.D.5. $12.

Taking of Property. 83 p. Sales No. E.00.II.D.4. $12.

National Treatment.. 94 p. Sales No. E.99.II.D.16. $12.

Admission and Establishment.. 69 p. Sales No. E.99.II.D.10. $12.

Trends in International Investment Agreements: An Overview. 133 p. Sales No. E.99.II.D.23. $12.

Lessons from the MAI. 52 p. Sales No. E.99.II.D.26. $10.

Fair and Equitable Treatment.. 85 p. Sales No. E.99.II.D.15. $12.

Transfer Pricing.. 71 p. Sales No. E.99.II.D.8. $12.

Scope and Definition. 93 p. Sales No. E.99.II.D.9. $12.

Most-Favoured Nation Treatment.. 57 p. Sales No. E.99.II.D.11. $12.
Investment-Related Trade Measures. 57 p. Sales No. E.99.II.D.12. $12.

Foreign Direct Investment and Development.. 74 p. Sales No. E.98.II.D.15. $12.

Investment Policy Monitors

Investment Policy Monitor. A Periodic Report by the UNCTAD Secretariat. No. 3, 7 October 2010.
http://www.unctad.org/en/docs/webdiaeia20105_en.pdf

Investment Policy Monitor. A Periodic Report by the UNCTAD Secretariat. No. 2, 20 April 2010.
http://www.unctad.org/en/docs/webdiaeia20102_en.pdf

Investment Policy Monitor. A Periodic Report by the UNCTAD Secretariat. No. 1, 4 December 2009.
http://www.unctad.org/en/docs/webdiaeia200911_en.pdf

IIA Monitors and Issues Notes

IIA Issues Note No. 1 (2010): Latest Developments in Investor–State Dispute Settlement.
http://www.unctad.org/en/docs/webdiaeia20103_en.pdf

IIA Monitor No. 3 (2009): Recent developments in international investment agreements (2008–June 2009).
http://www.unctad.org/en/docs/webdiaeia20098_en.pdf

IIA Monitor No. 2 (2009): Selected Recent Developments in IIA Arbitration and Human Rights.
http://www.unctad.org/en/docs/webdiaeia20097_en.pdf

IIA Monitor No. 1 (2009): Latest Developments in Investor–State Dispute Settlement.
http://www.unctad.org/en/docs/webdiaeia20096_en.pdf

IIA Monitor No. 2 (2008): Recent developments in international investment agreements (2007–June 2008).
http://www.unctad.org/en/docs/webdiaeia20081_en.pdf

IIA Monitor No. 1 (2008): Latest Developments in Investor– State Dispute Settlement.
http://www.unctad.org/en/docs/iteiia20083_en.pdf

IIA Monitor No. 3 (2007): Recent developments in international investment agreements (2006 – June 2007).
http://www.unctad.org/en/docs/webiteiia20076_en.pdf

IIA Monitor No. 2 (2007): Development implications of international investment agreements.
http://www.unctad.org/en/docs/webiteiia20072_en.pdf

IIA Monitor No. 1 (2007): Intellectual Property Provisions in International Investment Arrangements.
http://www.unctad.org/en/docs/webiteiia20071_en.pdf

IIA Monitor No. 4 (2006): Latest Developments in Investor-State Dispute Settlement.
http://www.unctad.org/sections/dite_pcbb/docs/webiteiia200611_en.pdf

IIA Monitor No. 3 (2006): The Entry into Force of Bilateral Investment Treaties (BITs).
http://www.unctad.org/en/docs/webiteiia20069_en.pdf

IIA Monitor No. 2 (2006): Developments in international investment agreements in 2005.
http://www.unctad.org/en/docs/webiteiia20067_en.pdf

IIA Monitor No. 1 (2006): Systemic Issues in International Investment Agreements (IIAs).
http://www.unctad.org/en/docs/webiteiia20062_en.pdf

IIA Monitor No. 4 (2005): Latest Developments in Investor-State Dispute Settlement.
http://www.unctad.org/en/docs/webiteiit20052_en.pdf

IIA Monitor No. 2 (2005): Recent Developments in International Investment Agreements.
http://www.unctad.org/en/docs/webiteiit20051_en.pdf

IIA Monitor No. 1 (2005): South-South Investment Agreements Proliferating.
http://www.unctad.org/en/docs/webiteiit20061_en.pdf

United Nations publications may be obtained from bookstores and distributors throughout the world. Please consult your bookstore or write:

For Africa, Asia and Europe to:

Sales Section
United Nations Office at Geneva
Palais des Nations
CH-1211 Geneva 10
Switzerland
Tel: (41-22) 917-1234
Fax: (41-22) 917-0123
E-mail: unpubli@unog.ch

For Asia and the Pacific, the Caribbean, Latin America and North America to:

Sales Section
Room DC2-0853
United Nations Secretariat
New York, NY 10017
United States
Tel: (1-212) 963-8302 or (800) 253-9646
Fax: (1-212) 963-3489
E-mail: publications@un.org

All prices are quoted in United States dollars.

For further information on the work of the Division on Investment and Enterprise, UNCTAD, please address inquiries to:

United Nations Conference on Trade and Development
Division on Investment and Enterprise
Palais des Nations, Room E-10054
CH-1211 Geneva 10, Switzerland
Telephone: (41-22) 917-5651
Telefax: (41-22) 917-0498
http://www.unctad.org

QUESTIONNAIRE

Most-Favoured-Nation Treatment: A Sequel
Sales No. E.10.II.D.19

In order to improve the quality and relevance of the work of the UNCTAD Division on Investment, Technology and Enterprise Development, it would be useful to receive the views of readers on this publication. It would therefore be greatly appreciated if you could complete the following questionnaire and return it to:

Readership Survey
UNCTAD Division on Investment and Enterprise
United Nations Office at Geneva
Palais des Nations, Room E-9123
CH-1211 Geneva 10, Switzerland
Fax: 41-22-917-0194

1. Name and address of respondent (optional):

   _____

   _____

2. Which of the following best describes your area of work?

Government	☐	Public enterprise	☐
Private enterprise	☐	Academic or research institution	☐
International organization	☐	Media	☐
Not-for-profit organization	☐	Other (specify) _____	

3. In which country do you work? _____

4.   What is your assessment of the contents of this publication?

Excellent   ☐   Adequate   ☐
Good   ☐   Poor   ☐

5.   How useful is this publication to your work?

Very useful   ☐   Somewhat useful   ☐
Irrelevant   ☐

6.   Please indicate the three things you liked best about this
     publication:

     _____

     _____

     _____

7.   Please indicate the three things you liked least about this
     publication:

     _____

     _____

     _____

8.   If you have read other publications of the UNCTAD Division on
     Investment, Enterprise Development and Technology, what is
     your overall assessment of them?

Consistently good   ☐   Usually good, but with
                               some exceptions   ☐
        Generally mediocre ☐   Poor   ☐

9. On average, how useful are those publications to you in your work?

    Very useful ☐ Somewhat useful ☐
    Irrelevant ☐

10. Are you a regular recipient of *Transnational Corporations* (formerly *The CTC Reporter*), UNCTAD-DITE's tri-annual refereed journal?

    Yes ☐ No ☐

    If not, please check here if you would like to receive a sample copy sent to the name and address you have given above: ☐